IS

# HELL

## FOR REAL OR DOES
## EVERYONE GO TO

# HEAVEN?

# IS
# HELL
## FOR REAL OR DOES EVERYONE GO TO
# HEAVEN?

CONTRIBUTORS

**TIMOTHY KELLER**     **R. ALBERT MOHLER, JR.**

**J. I. PACKER**     **ROBERT W. YARBROUGH**

GENERAL EDITORS

**CHRISTOPHER W. MORGAN**     **ROBERT A. PETERSON**

ZONDERVAN.com/
AUTHORTRACKER
*follow your favorite authors*

ZONDERVAN

*Is Hell for Real or Does Everyone Go to Heaven?*
Copyright © 2004, 2011 by Christopher W. Morgan and Robert A. Peterson

Parts of this book are adapted from *Hell Under Fire* and *The Art and Craft of Biblical Preaching*

This title is also available as a Zondervan ebook. Visit www.zondervan.com/ebooks.

Requests for information should be addressed to:

Zondervan, *Grand Rapids, Michigan 49530*

ISBN 978-0-310-49462-1

*Cover design: Rob Monacelli*
*Interior design: Matthew Van Zomeren*

*Printed in the United States of America*

11 12 13 14 15 16 /DCI/ 22 21 20 19 18 17 16 15 14 13 12 11 10 9 8 7 6 5 4 3 2 1

# CONTENTS

Preface . . . . . . . . . . . . . . . . . . . . . . . . . . . . . . . . . 7

1. **IS HELL FOR REAL?** . . . . . . . . . . . . . . . . 11
   R. Albert Mohler Jr.

2. **WHAT JESUS SAID ABOUT HELL** . . . 23
   Robert W. Yarbrough

3. **THREE PICTURES OF HELL** . . . . . . . . 37
   Christopher W. Morgan

4. **THREE PERSPECTIVES ON HELL** . . . 48
   Robert A. Peterson

5. **DOES EVERYONE GO TO HEAVEN?** . . 58
   J. I. Packer

Appendix: Preaching Hell in a Tolerant Age . . . . . . . 73
Timothy Keller

Conclusion . . . . . . . . . . . . . . . . . . . . . . . . . . . . . 81

Further Reading . . . . . . . . . . . . . . . . . . . . . . . . . 84

Notes . . . . . . . . . . . . . . . . . . . . . . . . . . . . . . . . . 85

Contributors . . . . . . . . . . . . . . . . . . . . . . . . . . . 89

# PREFACE

POPULAR MEDIA TOOK NOTE RECENTLY when one of film's most recognized and celebrated stars passed away. As a successful actress since the age of three, Elizabeth Taylor had virtually defined Hollywood's Golden Age, embodying an image of beauty for a generation of moviegoers. In later years, even though her many marriages became fodder for late-night talk show hosts, she became well-known for her humanitarian work on behalf of HIV and AIDS victims.

Sinner and saint, convert to Judaism, Taylor likely never professed faith in Jesus Christ. Dare one ask: Is she in hell now?

Two months later, the world's most notorious terrorist leader was killed by a team of U.S. operatives in suburban Abbottabad, Pakistan. Osama Bin Laden had eluded capture for nearly a decade, issuing periodic threats against Israel and the West by tapes leaked to Middle East news outlets. As the founder of Al Qaeda, his criminal résumé included numerous mass-casualty attacks, including the 9/11 plane crashes into the Pentagon and the World Trade Center.

Reviled and revered, a spokesperson for radical Islam, Bin Laden likely never professed faith in Jesus Christ. Is he in heaven now?

Asking such questions about people's eternal destinies tends to make most of us uncomfortable. Even more so, perhaps, when talking about those closer to home — a beloved relative, a former coworker or business associate, a longtime friend of the family. As the opening chapter of this book will show, looking too closely into someone's fate after death is, today, considered tasteless at best. At worst, it can appear hateful.

A book entitled *Who Goes There? A Cultural History of Heaven and Hell* found that our culture's outlook on the afterlife has evolved to the point where most now assume that the majority of people end up in a place or state of eternal bliss. Only a very few — the Pol Pots and Hitlers, the child molesters and pyramid-scheme architects — are thought to be elsewhere.

It comes as no surprise, then, that traditional Christian teaching on hell is under fire. The very idea of eternal, conscious torment for those apart from God runs in opposition to much of what the modern world values. So, too, does a wrathful God and any talk of judgment. So what are Christians to think?

During the months between the two deaths mentioned above, a firestorm of controversy and discussion erupted among evangelicals as a cover story in *Time* magazine raised the question in bold font "What if there's no hell?"[1] The spark was a book by a well-known American pastor questioning hell, but the underlying issues went far deeper than one controversial volume. Christians have been growing increasingly uncomfortable with hell for the past couple of centuries, and in light of our culture's intense distaste for it, believers are forced to at least consider dropping the doctrine. Would our public witness and our faithfulness to the God of love be better off without hell?

The task of this book is to answer that question. Featuring the contributions of several trusted pastors and theologians, it looks at the history of hell, the biblical teaching on it, and the implications of disposing with it. Fair disclosure, though: the contributors conclude that the church's historic teaching on hell must be maintained. What is lost by dispensing with hell, they find, is not just inferior to what is gained in the court of public opinion; it is also central to a right understanding of God, the gospel, humanity, and the purpose of life.

As such, the publisher's hope is that this book will provide readers with a simple, brief, and biblical explanation and defense of hell. Not only individual readers but groups as well might find it a helpful introduction to read, study, and discuss. The book covers the key issues under discussion in a straightforward way, as follows:

In chapter 1, seminary president R. Albert Mohler surveys the history of the doctrine in Western thought, showing why it has fallen from the prominent place it once held in the belief and imagination of God's people.

In chapter 2, New Testament professor Robert W. Yarbrough looks closely at what Jesus had to say about hell, finding that he spoke of it more often and with more severity than many Christians realize.

In chapter 3, theologian and author Christopher W. Morgan examines every teaching on hell in the New Testament, pulling out three aspects most emphasized by the biblical writers.

In chapter 4, theology professor Robert A. Peterson highlights the connection between hell and three key biblical themes.

In chapter 5, emeritus theologian J. I. Packer takes a direct and piercing look at *universalism* — that is, the teaching that everyone will eventually end up in heaven. He finds it wanting, suffering from poor biblical interpretation and internal inconsistencies.

Finally, an appendix from Manhattan pastor Timothy Keller provides suggestions for talking about hell amidst a tolerance-loving culture.

"To speak of hell is precarious. But not to speak of hell is more precarious," conclude the book's general editors. "We owe it to fellow sinners to tell them the unabridged story of [God's] love and forgiveness. That way they too can better understand their desperate need for forgiveness and experience the joy found only in knowing Christ."

May it be so, and may this book be a ready resource for readers looking for biblical answers to their questions about hell.

Paul E. Engle
*Senior Vice President and Publisher —*
*Church, Curriculum, Academic, and*
*Reference Resources*
*Zondervan*

# CHAPTER ONE

# IS HELL FOR REAL?

## R. ALBERT MOHLER JR.

On the whole, the disappearance of Hell was a great relief, though it brought new problems.

David Lodge, *Souls and Bodies*[2]

THE REJECTION OF CHRISTIANITY'S historic teaching on hell has come swiftly in our culture. It is now routinely dismissed as an embarrassing artifact from an ancient age — a reminder of Christianity's outdated worldview.

Yet the disappearance of hell within the church's walls, at least in some circles, presents a kind of mystery. How did such a central doctrine come to suffer widespread abandonment among some Christians?

The answer lies in the history of Christianity in the modern world, and it warns of further possible compromises on the horizon. For as the church has often been reminded, no doctrine stands alone. Take away hell, and the entire shape of Christian theology may be altered.

# HELL BEFORE THE MODERN WORLD

The church developed its teaching on hell during its very first centuries. Based on New Testament passages about eternal judgment and the afterlife, early preachers taught that hell was God's just judgment on sinners who did not put their faith in Christ. It was seen as real and eternal, characterized by fire and torment.

The first major challenge to this view came from a theologian named Origen, who taught that everyone and everything would ultimately be reconciled to God. He reasoned that God's victory could only be complete when nothing was left unredeemed, and that hell would not be eternal and punitive but rather temporary and purifying.

Origen's teaching was rejected by a church council held in Constantinople in AD 553, however, and the church's consensus on hell continued to be widely held for another thousand years. Rejections of hell during these years were limited to sects and heretics. Indeed, hell was such a fixture of the Christian mind that most persons understood all of life in terms of their ultimate destination. Men and women longed for heaven and feared hell.

The stark contrast between our modern distaste for hell and the premodern fascination with hell is evident in our sermons. A medieval Italian preacher warned his congregation against hell in this way:

> Fire, fire! That is the recompense for your perversity, you hardened sinners. Fire, fire, the fires of hell! Fire in your eyes, fire in your mouth, fire in your guts, fire in your throat, fire in your nostrils, fire inside and fire outside, fire beneath and fire above, fire in every part. Ah, miserable folk! You will be like rags burning in the middle of this fire.[3]

Jonathan Edwards, colonial America's great theologian and preacher, spoke similarly:

> Consider that if once you get into hell, you'll never get out. If you should unexpectedly one of these days drop in there; [there] would be no remedy. They that go there return no more. Consider how dread-

ful it will be to suffer such an extremity forever. It is dreadful beyond expression to suffer it half an hour. O the misery, the tribulation and anguish that is endured![4]

Few congregations would hear such warnings today. A preacher who spoke so graphically about hell might be considered eccentric or worse. This change in churches' sermons and in the sensibilities underlying them began during the periods of Western history that historians call the Renaissance and the Enlightenment.

## QUESTIONS ABOUT HELL

During the seventeenth century, even as Europe continued to be a largely Christian continent, various streams of atheism and skepticism emerged.

The Socinians, for instance, taught that Jesus was not fully God and that his death was not needed for the forgiveness of sins. They also questioned the eternality of punishment in hell, teaching instead that the wicked would be destroyed in hell—a view that has come to be known as annihilationism. Eternal torment was an unjust penalty for a short human lifetime of sins, they reasoned.

Groups like the Socinians were far enough outside of the mainstream to have little influence on the larger church. However, their thinking resonated with the educated elite. Many came to doubt hell's existence, even if they felt it was a useful teaching to maintain social order.

As D. P. Walker has written in *The Decline of Hell*:

People who had doubts about the eternity of hell, or who had come to disbelieve in it, refrained from publishing their doubts not only because of the personal risk involved, but also because of genuine moral scruples. In the 17th century disbelief in eternal torment seldom reached the level of a firm conviction, but at the most was a conjecture, which one might wish to be true; it was therefore understandable that one should hesitate to plunge the world into moral anarchy for the sake of only conjectural truth.[5]

R. ALBERT MOHLER JR.

In the eighteenth century, Enlightenment skepticism took center stage. Philosophers began arguing that hell should be viewed metaphorically, not literally. Alternately, Thomas Hobbes suggested in *Leviathan* that hell might be eternal, but the torments of the unsaved were not—another version of the Socinians' annihilationism. Voltaire and the other atheistic philosophers rejected Christianity entirely.

## A CRISIS OF FAITH

These stirrings against Christian doctrine remained largely outside the church, however, until the Victorian era, a period of time in the nineteenth century often sentimentalized for its Christian vitality. Queen Victoria of England was an emblem of Christian devotion, and Christianity was part of the very fabric of the expanding British Empire. Attendance at churches both rural and urban reached an all-time high, with great churches such as Charles Spurgeon's Metropolitan Tabernacle drawing thousands.

Yet Spurgeon's traditional doctrines were not shared by all Victorians. Indeed, during a famous sermon at Oxford University in 1833, John Keble lamented the era as a "discouraged epoch, where the faith is completely dead or dying."[6] Though many Britons of the nineteenth century maintained a robust faith, historian Jaroslav Pelikan has written that the age also produced "radical doubt" and "the negation of dogma."[7]

Among many Victorians, hell became something of an obsession. A rejection of the church's traditional view extended throughout the leaders of society, including statesmen like the high-churchman Prime Minister William Gladstone, who asserted that hell had been "relegated ... to the far-off corners of the Christian mind ... there to sleep in the deep shadow as a thing needless in our enlightened and progressive age."[8]

The story of Leslie Stephen, the father of novelist Virginia Woolf, captures well the spirit of the age. An ordained clergyman in the

Church of England, Stephen lost his faith, renounced his ordination, and became a man of learning. Various strains of philosophy had undermined the foundations of Christian conviction for him, and he came to see Victorian Christianity as hypocritical:

> The average Cambridge don of my day was (as I thought and think) a sensible and honest man who wished to be both rational and Christian. He was rational enough to see that the old orthodox position was untenable. He did not believe in hell, or in "verbal inspiration" [of Scripture].... He thought that the controversies on such matters were silly and antiquated, and spoke of them with indifference, if not with contempt. But he also thought that religious belief of some kind was necessary or valuable, and considered himself to be a genuine believer.[9]

Other literary figures shared Stephen's rejection of hell. Consider Lewis Carroll, for instance, the famous author of *Alice in Wonderland*. Born Charles Lutwidge Dodgson —Carroll was a pen name— he was the son of an Anglican minister. Though in other respects a faithful Anglican, Dodgson held what one biographer called an "instinctive repugnance" for the doctrine of everlasting punishment.

Influenced by new critical views of Scripture, Dodgson declared that if the Bible really taught the doctrine of everlasting punishment, "I would give up the Bible." After his death, Dodgson left behind an unpublished manuscript entitled "Eternal Punishment,"[10] in which he presented what he thought was an airtight logical case against hell. He argued that the goodness of God is preeminent and that biblical teaching on hell can be discounted because the idea that God inspired the Bible's very words "has been largely modified in these days."

One of the most popular Victorian preachers acknowledged that his congregation had "learned to smile" at the idea of an eternal hell, for "in bodily awful intolerable torture we believe no longer." A chaplain to Queen Victoria went so far as to label hell a "blasphemy against the merciful God."[11]

By the end of the Victorian era, poet Thomas Hardy could imagine himself observing God's funeral. The Victorian crisis of faith spread throughout the aristocracy and the educated classes, and theologians and preachers added their voices to the calls for changes to traditional Christian teaching. Hell was at the center of their attention. Whereas preachers in earlier eras were concerned to save persons from punishment in hell, many Victorian preachers wanted to save their congregations from the fear of hell.

One other aspect of the Victorian mind-set is important. The Victorian ideal of family life featured a loving, respected, upright father. Such a father would discipline his children, but never severely. Eventually, he would bring punishment to an end, leading to reconciliation. When this vision of fatherhood was extended to God, hell as eternal torment became unthinkable.

Yet like the Enlightenment elites before them, Victorians wanted to retain and reinforce moral order in society, and belief in hell was considered to be a key restraint on what is now commonly called antisocial behavior. For this reason, some Victorians retained hell as socially important, even when they no longer believed it to be real. As historian Geoffrey Rowell has written, "the need of hell as a moral sanction, and the underlying sense that, however crudely expressed and distorted the doctrine might be, it did attempt to state something of importance about ultimate ethical issues, meant that it could not be quietly discarded."[12]

Throughout the Victorian era, currents of theological change were also evident in America. Growing numbers of Deists and Unitarians rejected the idea of God as judge. In certain circles, "higher criticism" of the Bible undermined confidence in it as God's revelation, and pastors increasingly treated hell as a metaphor. The nation's seminaries and mainline churches became marked by a liberal theology that denied historic doctrines. Influential Brooklyn pastor Henry Ward Beecher, for instance, rejected the old orthodoxy specifically for what he called its "spiritual barbarism" and "hideous doctrines" — doctrines like the eternal punishment of the unsaved in hell.

Victorian-era doubts about historic Christian beliefs were not limited to hell, though. As Western nations colonized countries around the world, Westerners confronted other people's gods, practices, and worldviews. This discovery led some Victorian thinkers to emphasize the universal fatherhood of God, and they came up with ways to soften Christianity's claim of salvation through Christ alone. In Germany, a "history of religions" school of thought treated Christianity as just one form of human religion alongside others, with all religions understood to be human inventions.

Above all, when they thought about God, Victorians increasingly came to the conclusion that he was universally benevolent. This concept of a humanitarian God would have doctrinal repercussions in the twentieth century.

## HELL IN THE TWENTIETH CENTURY

"The cosmology of the New Testament is essentially mythical in character," declared German theologian Rudolf Bultmann in the mid-twentieth century, and such a mythological worldview is "unacceptable to modern man whose thinking has been shaped by science."[13] According to Bultmann, Christianity therefore needed to revise its claims in order to better fit the modern mind-set — including any claim that hell was real and a threat.

Simultaneously a time of great technological advancement and great evil, the twentieth century saw many Christian theologians focused on making Christianity relevant to modern humanity's worldview and needs. The interminable trench warfare of World War I had established new benchmarks for carnage on the battlefield, bringing the nineteenth-century's faith in human progress to a collapse. What World War I did not destroy, World War II took by assault and atrocity. The battlefields of Verdun and Ypres gave way to the ovens of Dachau and Auschwitz as symbols of the century.

At the same time, the technological revolutions of the century led to an outlook that gave science and the natural world preeminence, with spiritual truths relegated to mere personal or speculative interest. As a result, the place of religion was diminished in the public sphere. Secularization became the norm in Western societies, alongside advanced technologies and ever-increasing wealth.

Both heaven and hell thus took on an essentially this-worldly character for liberal Christians. If the atrocities of the Holocaust represented hell on earth, what fear did secular moderns have of a hell to come? If the blessings of material abundance were so readily available to some, what solace was promised by the hope of heaven?

Theologians such as Reinhold Niebuhr came to see hell in the impoverished ghettos of inner city America. Karl Barth held out hope that the victory of God in Christ would lead to universal salvation. Jürgen Moltmann wrote, "Salvation is not another world in the 'beyond.' It means that this world becomes finally different."[14] Thus, heaven became liberation and hell oppression for many liberal Christians.

By the end of the century, many liberal Christians had abandoned claims of exclusivity for the Christian faith. In accommodating themselves to the secular and antisupernatural worldview of the times, belief in a literal hell became incredible and unacceptable— an embarrassment to the Christian faith.

## A FEW EVANGELICALS JOIN THE DEBATE

Despite Victorian-era questions about hell and twentieth century reimagining of it, evangelical Christians tended to believe and preach the traditional doctrine. What Charles Spurgeon preached about hell in 1855 would have been upheld by most evangelicals a century later:

> Suffice it for me to close up by saying, that the hell of hells will be to thee poor sinner, the thought, that it is to be *forever*. Thou wilt look up there on the throne of God, and it shall be written "For ever!" When the damned jingle the burning irons of their torments, they shall say, "for ever!" When they howl, echo cries "for ever!"[15]

Spurgeon was hardly unaware of the denials of hell common in his age. He had seen his theology parodied in the novels of George Eliot and Charles Kingsley. He knew that many Victorians viewed hell as nothing more than a metaphor, but he would not have it:

> Now, do not begin telling me that that is metaphorical fire: who cares for that? If a man were to threaten to give me a metaphorical blow on the head, I should care very little about it; he would be welcome to give me as many as he pleased. And what say the wicked? "We do not care about metaphorical fires." But they are *real*, sir—yes, as real as yourself. There is a real fire in hell, as truly as you now have a real body—a fire exactly like that which we have on earth in everything except this—that it will not consume, though it will torture you.[16]

Similarly, evangelicals throughout the twentieth century knew of society's and liberal Christians' critiques. Nevertheless, pastors on both sides of the Atlantic continued to make hell a major focus of their preaching.

In the 1970s and 1980s, challenges to the traditional doctrine finally moved into evangelicalism. John Wenham, a British Bible scholar, issued a call to reconsider an aspect of hell in 1974.[17] Wenham leaned toward the annihilationist view that unbelievers might be destroyed rather than endlessly tortured in hell, but he warned that the traditional view should not be given up lightly. "The temptation to twist what may be quite plain statements of Scripture is intense," he wrote. "It is the ideal situation for unconscious rationalizing."[18]

By 1991, Wenham had come to fully support annihilationism, which he described as the belief "that God created Man only potentially immortal."[19] Those apart from Christ, in this view, would not be given the gift of eternal life but would pass from existence after judgment.

Wenham's viewpoint on hell's duration was shared by John Stott, a widely respected evangelical leader. Stott said that the church had misunderstood the meaning of key biblical texts. In Matthew 10:28, for instance, Stott said that the Greek word for *destroy* meant complete destruction rather than everlasting punishment.

Stott also claimed that biblical imagery such as the "lake of fire" in Revelation 20 was not intended to suggest eternal torment for unbelieving humans. "Would there not [otherwise] ... be a serious disproportion between sins consciously committed in time and torment consciously experienced throughout eternity?" he wondered.[20]

In America, the late theologian Clark Pinnock also began arguing both for annihilationism and for a future opportunity for those who had never heard of Christ to respond to him after death. By the end of the twentieth century, though the vast majority of evangelicals still upheld the church's historic doctrine of hell, some had begun to question aspects of it.

## UNDERLYING CULTURAL TRENDS

Christian thinker Os Guinness has noted that Western societies "have reached the state of pluralization where choice is not just a state of affairs, it is a state of mind.... To be modern is to be addicted to choice and change."[21] In such a context, Christian teaching can easily be driven by cultural currents.

What specific currents have led some evangelicals today to reimagine hell? The answer comes down to the problem of evil—specifically, how a good God could allow sin yet still blame humans for it—and to four related issues.

*The first issue is a changed view of God.* The biblical vision of God has largely been rejected by our culture as offensive and restrictive to human freedom. Thus, some evangelicals now promote a divine love that is never coercive and would never sentence anyone—however guilty—to eternal torment and anguish.

It is surely easier to persuade secular persons to believe in a God who never judges than to believe in the God preached by Jonathan Edwards or Charles Spurgeon. But is this way of connecting with our contemporary culture a risk to genuine biblical convictions? As was mentioned earlier, modern persons want God to embody current human standards of righteousness and love. But what if such standards contradict biblical standards at various points?

*The second issue is a changed view of justice.* Retributive justice, meaning the punishment of wrongdoing, has been the hallmark of human law since premodern times. It assumes that punishment is natural and necessary. However, this idea has been under assault for many years in Western cultures, which has led to much discomfort about hell.

Rejecting universal moral standards, philosophers such as John Stuart Mill argued that justice is about restoration rather than retribution. Criminals came to be seen not as deserving punishment but as needing correction. The goal was rehabilitation. Yet this shift from the prison to the penitentiary was rejected by C. S. Lewis as a threat to the very concept of justice:

> Thus when we cease to consider what the criminal deserves and consider only what will cure him or deter others, we have tacitly removed him from the sphere of justice altogether; instead of a person, a subject of rights, we now have a mere object, a patient, a "case."[22]

As the transformation of legal practice has redefined justice, some theologians have incorporated this new view into their doctrines of hell. For Roman Catholics, for instance, the doctrine of purgatory functions as a kind of penitentiary. Similarly for some evangelicals, a view of hell as temporary and corrective—rather than eternal and punitive—has become the remedy.

*The third issue is the advent of a psychological worldview.* Human behavior is increasingly understood by psychological views that, intended or not, can reduce personal responsibility. Various theories blame human wrongdoing on external influences, genetics, the influence of the subconscious, and so on.

In a psychological age, being true to one's self can become the ultimate goal, and wrongdoings may be excused as either growth experiences or "personal issues." Shame and guilt are repressive and need to be overcome. Amid such a worldview, the finality of God's sentencing of sinners to hell is all but unthinkable.

*The fourth issue is a changed concept of salvation.* Most men and women throughout Western history awoke in the morning and went to sleep at night with hell never far from their consciousness—until now. Sin has largely been redefined as personal failings rather than an insult to God; therefore, salvation has come to be seen as liberation from oppression, either internal or external. Within this understanding, the gospel has become a means of release from bad habits rather than a rescue from hell.

Yet these four issues are only part of the picture. The most basic cause of the controversy over hell is the question it poses to God's goodness. When Christians limit salvation to those who put their faith in Christ during their earthly lives, modern persons question God's character. To the modern mind, this gospel message sounds unfair and discriminatory. Some evangelicals have responded by saying that hell is either nonexistent or hardly populated.

Churches that have not redefined hell have occasionally recast the gospel message instead. In a study of seeker-sensitive churches, researcher Kimon Howland Sargeant noted that "today's cultural pluralism fosters an under-emphasis on the 'hard sell' of Hell while contributing to an overemphasis on the 'soft sell' of personal satisfaction through Jesus Christ."[23] In other words, many churches now talk about new life in Christ without talking about judgment apart from him.

The temptation to revise the doctrine of hell is understandable—and in light of Western history, perhaps unavoidable. However, as the rest of the chapters in this book will show, it is a temptation that we should seek to resist. That is because hell is not a theological trifle, but rather an essential part of the biblical story about life, God, and the humanity he created in his image.

# CHAPTER TWO

# WHAT JESUS SAID ABOUT HELL

## ROBERT W. YARBROUGH

THROUGHOUT CHURCH HISTORY, Christians generally thought that Jesus' teaching included not only a joyful message but also a severe warning. Specifically, he was believed to have said that those who oppose God or spurn the gospel of salvation in his name will be consigned to hell at some point following earthly death, there to face a misery without end. Yet some are now insisting that Jesus said the wicked will cease to exist after death rather than undergo eternal conscious suffering — or that he will eventually reconcile all of humanity, repentant or not, to himself.

Because Jesus is the central authority for Christians, his teachings are of utmost significance. So which is true? Does the historic view find support in Jesus' teaching or do the new views? This chapter will show that Jesus' teaching actually bears much of the burden for the historic belief, and that his words are an insurmountable hurdle for revisionists to overcome.

# A PRELIMINARY QUESTION

However, one key question must be answered first: Can we really know what Jesus said about anything? Ever since the Enlightenment in the late eighteenth century, skepticism about the truthfulness of the four Gospels has increased, first in literary and academic circles and then gradually extending to the general public.

One recent example of this low respect for the Gospels was the Jesus Seminar, a maverick collection of scholars who claimed that only a small percentage of Jesus' words in the Gospels were actually said by him. The work of this group has been exposed as tendentious and unconvincing. But the corrosive effects of over two centuries of assault on the Gospels is not easily undone.

In such a climate it is tempting to question the Gospels' teaching on hell. Perhaps the words they attribute to Jesus are actually later church teachings projected back by well-meaning but misguided writers. Perhaps Jesus' words are relative in meaning and open to reinterpretation, particularly since they refer to things beyond the space-time world as we know it. Or maybe Christianity, contrary to age-old convention, is simply free to rethink what used to be nonnegotiable teachings. What harm can there be in jettisoning a presumably less important, difficult doctrine like an eternal hell if doing so draws more people to the Christian message?

The problem is that if Jesus did speak frequently and directly about hell, as the Gospel writers claim, then we may lose the Christian message if we modify his doctrine of hell. This is not the place to embark on a full defense of the Bible's truthfulness—other books have done that well—but it bears noting that every generation is tempted to redefine Scripture to fit the times. We should be wary of the current impulse to dilute Jesus' words on hell.

As North Park University professor Scot McKnight has written, "What Christians have believed about hell has been constructed almost entirely out of" what Jesus teaches in the Gospels.[24] If his words about hell are set aside, then nearly all of his teachings must be neutralized. We could be seeing that take place in current discussions on the subject. That is why we need to look again at Jesus' teaching on eternal punishment.

## WHAT JESUS SAID

Let us examine every passage in the Gospels in which Jesus speaks of hell, noting the main thrust of what he says from nine vantage points.

### 1. The Sermon on the Mount

Jesus gives a central place to hell in his best-known recorded sermon (Matt. 5–7). He warns against hateful anger, because "anyone who says, 'You fool!' will be in danger of the fire of hell" (5:22). He warns against adulterous looks and actions, lecherous sins of the eye and hand. Gouge out the eye, cut off the hand, Jesus says, because "it is better for you to lose one part of your body than for your whole body to be thrown into hell" (5:29–30). Although it is widely agreed that he overstates here for rhetorical effect, even as a figure of speech his words are graphic.

Later in his ministry Jesus repeats these statements in a different connection (18:9), and he makes it clear that hell involves a fire that never ends: "It is better for you to enter life maimed or crippled than to have two hands or two feet and be thrown into eternal fire" (18:8). He makes it clear that people face vastly different eternal destinies: "Enter through the narrow gate. For wide is the gate and broad is the road that leads to destruction, and many enter through it. But small is the gate and narrow the road that leads to life, and only a few find it" (7:13–14).

Such passages suggest that Jesus viewed hell as real, awful, and "eternal" (we will discuss the meaning of this word more fully below). Jesus also used the fear of hell as a motivator, inciting people to take painful measures now, if necessary, to avoid a fate worse than mere physical death later.

## 2. Jesus' Teaching When Commissioning His Disciples

When Jesus sent out the Twelve, he realized they would be harassed, hated, and persecuted. The temptation to cowardice or compromise would be strong. Jesus' own example of courage under fire was one incentive for them to take to heart: "A student is not above the teacher, nor a servant above his master.... If the head of the house has been called Beelzebul, how much more the members of his household!" (Matt. 10:24–25). Yet Jesus gave them another incentive as well: the fear of God, whose disapproval is more terrible than any harm inflicted by people. In this connection Christ states: "Do not be afraid of those who kill the body but cannot kill the soul. Rather, be afraid of the One who can destroy both soul and body in hell" (10:28).

Once again we see Christ appeal to hell, this time as a positive motivator to grasp the nettle of Christian service boldly even when it involves loss, pain, and earthly destruction. Temporary discomfort here and now is preferable to permanent calamity in the age to come.

## 3. Jesus' Teaching about the Destiny of His Opponents

The passages above were addressed to his disciples. But Jesus extends this grim prospect to those who oppose his message, including the religious leaders of Jerusalem and Judea. He calls these leaders "hypocrites," in part because by opposing him they "shut the door of the kingdom of heaven in people's faces" (Matt. 23:13). Jesus accused them of turning people away from his message, producing a convert who is then "twice as much a child of hell" as they themselves (23:15).

In biblical usage the term "child/son of" usually means physical descendent. But it also has a metaphorical meaning. "A child of hell" is someone whose life shows the same qualities as the religious leaders. Here Jesus' teaching implies that hell exerts influence on people to remain in their natural, unsaved moral condition rather than responding with a whole heart to Jesus' call to repentance and personal trust in him. Hell is thus a sphere of influence in the present world as well as a destination in the world to come.

## 4. The Gospels of Mark and Luke

All the references so far come from Matthew. But other Gospels include identical words from Jesus on hell. Jesus also speaks of hell in Luke's gospel in the story of the rich man and Lazarus: "In Hades, where he [the rich man] was in torment, he looked up and saw Abraham far away, with Lazarus by his side" (Luke 16:23). This parable is not intended to provide a detailed geography of hell. Yet the picture of an impious sinner tortured by thirst and anxiety fits what Jesus says about hell throughout the Gospels. There is no reason to suppose that Jesus speaks of hell differently in this parable than he does in Matthew. Significantly, this passage points again to conscious and unending torment endured by people in hell.

In the gospel of Mark, John asks Jesus what to do about people who cast out demons in Jesus' name but are not part of the Twelve. Jesus replies with a threefold answer. (1) Disciples must go to any lengths necessary to be at peace with each other (cf. Mark 9:50) rather than please themselves and as a result "go into hell, where the fire never goes out" (9:43). (2) It is preferable, Jesus goes on to say, "to enter life crippled than to have two feet and be thrown into hell" (9:45). (3) Finally, "it is better for you to enter the kingdom of God with one eye than to have two eyes and be thrown into hell, where 'the worms that eat them do not die, and the fire is not quenched'" (9:47–48).

Jesus makes a point in this passage to emphasize the unending nature of hell's affliction. He does this, first, by speaking of the "fire [that] never goes out." Then he does it by quoting Isaiah 66:24, one of two Old Testament passages that clearly teach about eternal punishment (see also Dan. 12:2). Jesus endorses this Old Testament view when he appropriates these teachings as part of his own.

## 5. The Gospel of John

John's gospel does not contain the word "hell." But Jesus does mention unending affliction in it: "Whoever believes in the Son has eternal life, but whoever rejects the Son will not see life, for God's wrath remains on them" (John 3:36). Virtually everyone agrees that "eternal life" in this passage refers to unending blessedness in God's presence. But some wish to shorten "God's wrath" to a limited time or experience. In their view, wrath "remains" but is not experienced consciously, despite other passages in John in which the same Greek word likely connotes everlasting duration (see 6:27, 56; 8:35; 12:34).

The evidence throughout John's gospel makes this unlikely, however. Jesus often juxtaposes "eternal life" with a cluster of negative expressions: "perish" (John 3:16; 10:28), "condemned" (3:18; 5:24, 28), "judgment" (5:22, 30), "death" (5:24), and "die" (6:50). The blessed state of eternal life is logically opposite to the condemned state of eternal destruction. If salvation and conscious bliss are everlasting, so too are perdition and conscious torment.

Overall, we must understand Jesus' references to perishing, dying, and destruction in light of his clear teaching on eternal conscious punishment.

## 6. The Meaning of "Eternal" in Jesus' Teaching

There is a minority view that claims when Jesus says the word "eternal," he means an unending experience in heaven but an unending effect in hell—that is, believers enjoy heaven forever whereas unbelievers are destroyed and cease to exist forever. This view goes back several centuries. In response to it, I will simply cite one of North America's earliest Bible scholars, Moses Stuart, who already in 1830 had carefully examined the issue and arrived at this conclusion:

> The result seems to be plain, and philologically and exegetically certain. It is this; either the declarations of the Scriptures do not establish the facts, that God and his glory and praise and happiness are endless; nor that the happiness of the righteous in a future world is endless; or else they establish the fact, [and] that the punishment of the wicked is endless. The whole stand or fall together. There can, in the very nature of antithesis, be no room for rational doubt here, in what manner we should interpret the declarations of the sacred writers. WE MUST EITHER ADMIT THE ENDLESS

28

MISERY OF HELL, OR GIVE UP THE ENDLESS HAPPINESS OF HEAVEN.[25]

### 7. So What Did Jesus Teach About Hell?

To summarize, Jesus' words on hell seem fairly straightforward. There will be a bodily resurrection of all persons, the good and the wicked (John 5:28–29). The good (those who have received Jesus and his saving message) will enter heaven. This is a place of blessing and unending joy in the presence of God. The wicked (those who have not received Christ's saving message) will enter hell: "Then they will go away to eternal punishment, but the righteous to eternal life" (Matt. 25:46). The symmetry is stark and simple. As McKnight concludes, Jesus clearly teaches "punishment in an individual, eternal sense."[26]

We have seen that Jesus depicted hell as real, awful, everlasting, motivational, and influential in this life. In view of modern doubts about hell, Jesus' clear teaching is all the more helpful.

### 8. Echoes of Jesus' Teaching Elsewhere in the New Testament

Jesus' teaching about hell is found in the Gospels. But in a sense the whole of the New Testament can be seen as coming from Jesus, since writers like Paul claimed to be passing along or applying his teaching. If some people choose to minimize individual gospel passages on hell, the evidence of other passages by other writers—all followers of Jesus claiming to pass along his divine teaching and not their own—still remains. Jesus' early followers taught nothing different on hell from their Master. Some New Testament books, especially Hebrews and Revelation, extend aspects of Jesus' teaching on hell.

### 9. The Old Testament Foundation of Jesus' Teaching

Furthermore, as mentioned earlier, what Jesus teaches about the afterlife corresponds with the Old Testament. There is a direct connection between Jesus' words about eternal life and the hope of Abraham, Moses, and Isaiah. The entire Old Testament testifies to an eternal reward for God's people and to a corollary eternal misery for those apart from God. While Jesus builds on Old Testament teaching—and corrects those who were out of sync with it—he does not contradict it.

The Old Testament passages are most emphatic. In Isaiah 66:24, the prophet writes, "And they will go out and look on the dead bodies of those who rebelled against me; the worms that eat them will not die, and the fire that burns them not be quenched, and they will be loathsome to all mankind." Similarly, Daniel 12:2 reads, "Multitudes who sleep in the dust of the earth will awake: some to everlasting life, others to shame and everlasting contempt."

Just as we can be sure that the Messiah promised in the Old Testament offers eternal life and has prepared an eternal abode for his people in heaven (John 14:2–3), so we can also be sure that he spoke knowledgeably and authoritatively about the everlasting woes of hell he urged all to avoid.

## A DIFFERENT UNDERSTANDING OF JESUS' TEACHING

Houston lawyer Edward W. Fudge has become well-known for advocating the view mentioned earlier that when the wicked die, their punishment is eternal death rather than eternal torment. This view is called conditional immortality or annihilationism. Fudge writes:

> The fact is that the Bible does not teach the traditional view of final punishment. Scripture nowhere suggests that God is an eternal torturer. It never says the damned will writhe in ceaseless torment or that the glories of heaven will forever be blighted by the screams from hell. The idea of conscious everlasting torment was a grievous mistake, a horrible error, a gross slander against the heavenly Father, whose character we truly see in the life of Jesus of Nazareth.[27]

Some of Fudge's language may be set aside as heated rhetoric. The historic view does not see God as "an eternal torturer" but rather as a righteous judge (see Rom. 3:5–6). Heaven will not "forever be blighted by the screams from hell," but will rather be a place with "no more death or mourning or crying or pain, for the old order of things has passed away" (Rev. 21:4). Without giving all of the details, Scripture promises that hell's woes will not mar heaven's blessedness.

More importantly, to call belief in conscious everlasting punishment "a grievous mistake, a horrible error, a gross slander against the heavenly Father" is a risky charge in light of the words of Jesus on hell. Jesus speaks clearly about the "traditional" view that Fudge associates with slander of God.

In order to refute Fudge's view, let's look at a couple of key passages in which he offers an interpretation very different from the traditional one.

"Do not be afraid of those who kill the body but cannot kill the soul. Rather, be afraid of the One who can destroy both soul and body in hell" (Matt. 10:28). Fudge stresses that "kill" and "destroy" are parallel, and he understands "destroy" to mean annihilate. So Jesus' warning is to fear God because he can make both soul and body cease to exist any longer.[28]

However, it makes better sense to understand Jesus' warning as it has historically been understood. Matthew 10 is about Jesus' sending out the Twelve. They will face danger, treachery, and things like flogging (10:17). They will be tempted to be cowardly rather than face pain or even death. But there is a second death more fearful than any earthly end. God is able to inflict an unending misery on the whole person, "soul and body." We say "unending" for two reasons.

First, Jesus in a similar passage calls this affliction "eternal" (remember the discussion above), and there is no compelling reason to interpret a death Jesus calls eternal elsewhere as temporary here.

Second, "destroy" in the New Testament can sometimes refer to enduring torment. For instance, the unclean spirits who ask whether Jesus will "destroy" them (Mark 1:24; Luke 4:34) are clearly not afraid of death or even temporary torment. Rather, they fear that Jesus might begin the "forever and ever" torment that the book of Revelation says is the destiny of the devil and all those loyal to him (Rev. 14:11), including unclean spirits.

Taken alone, this one passage may be inconclusive, however. So let's look at another one. "It is better for you to enter the kingdom of God with one eye than to have two eyes and be thrown into hell, where 'the worms that eat them do not die, and the fire is not quenched'" (Mark 9:47–48).

In dealing with this verse, Fudge sticks to his guns: "The devouring worm is aided by unquenchable fire that cannot be put out and that therefore continues to destroy until nothing remains." He appeals to a reading of Isaiah 66:24, which Jesus quotes in this passage, that sees in the worm and fire imagery corpses that decompose or are burned into oblivion.

This is an unlikely interpretation of Isaiah's meaning. For one thing, the logic is strained. A fire that "continues to destroy until nothing remains" is not unquenchable; instead, it goes out after everything is burned up.

Furthermore, destruction cannot be completed and at the same time "last for all eternity." Fudge speculates that Jesus (and Isaiah) is referring to worm and fire left over after destruction, but that is not what Jesus says. Rather, he refers to the ongoing ravages of maggots and flames. The grotesqueness of the image and the sternness of the warning are dependent on such horrors being ongoing.

As biblical scholar Peter Head shows, this understanding of the passage in Isaiah prevailed during Jesus' lifetime and can be seen in Jewish and Greek texts like Judith, 1 Enoch, and the *Sibylline Oracles*.[29] It is the most natural and straightforward reading of what Jesus says in Mark.

## DID EARLY CHRISTIANS MISINTERPRET JESUS' WORDS ON HELL?

Another overarching objection of Fudge's is worth examining, too. He maintains that the Greek or Platonic idea that all souls are immortal caused ancient Christians like Augustine to conclude that those in hell could never die. Jesus, according to Fudge, never teaches that all souls are immortal.

Fudge is correct that early Christian writers typically believed hell's punishments would be unending. They were saying so three hundred years before Augustine. Yet it was biblical reasons, not philosophical ones, that prompted this belief. One early Christian book called *The Epistle of Barnabas*, for instance, speaks both of eternal punishment and of bodily resurrection — the latter concept being laughable for most Greeks.

Indeed, it would be several hundred years before a Christian writer would put forward Fudge's view. Arnobius did so in the early fourth century, and his teaching on hell was subsequently deemed heretical by a church council in 553 and again in 1513. Rather than charging earlier Christians with following Plato and crediting Arnobius alone for understanding Jesus correctly, perhaps we should side with the vast majority of early Christians on what Jesus' words about hell meant.

Furthermore, while early Christians did borrow from Greek thinking, it is worth noting their many biblical convictions that had no place in Platonism, including:

- the uniqueness of Jesus Christ as the divine and human Son of God
- the necessity of personal faith in his death and resurrection for salvation
- the resurrection of the body, both of Christ and of all persons following death
- the doctrine of creation, to say nothing of creation out of nothing
- the future thousand-year reign of Christ
- the authority of the Old and New Testaments over human reason
- the tie between religion and morality
- the creation of humans in God's image
- the special place of the Hebrew people in God's plan of salvation
- the doctrine of original sin

It was Jesus' words in the Scriptures, not Plato's writings, that gave the church the discomfiting doctrine of hell. As one church historian has observed, early Christians "generally, in spite of a good deal of confusion, are on their guard against the current Platonic theory of immortality."[30] No doubt the church, then and now, has erred in many ways — particularly at times in the spirit with which it has upheld the historic doctrine of hell. But it has not been unfaithful to Jesus in believing what he taught about it.

## "COMPASSIONATE" OBJECTIONS TO HELL

As the previous chapter showed, disenchantment with the historic view of hell has been rising for several centuries, and among evangelicals John Stott in 1988 lent legitimacy to the annihilationist view. "I find the concept [of eternal conscious torment] intolerable," he wrote, "and do not understand how people can live with it without cauterizing their feelings or cracking under the strain."[31]

Stott's admission has had an incalculable influence among the international evangelical community, which looks to him and leaders like him for guidance. While most Christians can empathize with his compassionate angst about hell, our study above justifies several observations in response.

First, if most New Testament scholars and early church writers are headed in the right direction, then Jesus did not find the concept of eternal conscious punishment intolerable. On the contrary, it was much on his mind and on his lips. Yet his feelings were not cauterized, and while the pressures he faced were enormous, he did not crack under the strain.

If Jesus passed on this teaching without it driving him to distraction, we can assume that he felt his followers would be able to bear it with comparable solemnity, trusting in the God who both loves and judges while seeking the salvation of sinners like themselves. Jesus' followers are to go into the world teaching all the things that he commanded (Matt. 28:20). There is no reason to suppose that he granted them a bye when it came to the doctrine of hell. Nor do Jesus' words allow for a time to come when Christians more humane than he might be permitted to improve on his too-stern beliefs.

Second, while Stott's warning about emotional hardening is praiseworthy, another timely warning would be against the moral vertigo of much of contemporary Western culture. Along with the modern and postmodern loss of transcendence has come the demise of a strong sense of right and wrong. There is little ethical firm ground now.

Meanwhile, barbarity of all descriptions rages on many fronts and may even be growing worse, from child abuse to Internet porn to abortion to idolatrous consumerism to murderous racial and ethnic struggles. These things are not hell, but they are hellish symptoms of the human condition. Jesus spoke of a time when "because of the increase of wickedness, the love of most will grow cold" (Matt. 24:12). Have we sought to replace God with a weak policeman who would never pronounce an eternal sentence against such evil?

Having just emerged from a century in which 187 million people were killed by war and war-related causes, we cannot suppose that we are more moral than people in past eras. We have to face the possibility that the current desire to reform the doctrine of hell could be a sign of misguided sentimentality rather than the discovery of a truer meaning in Jesus' words.

When it comes to our feelings cracking under the strain of an eternal conscious hell, I would reply that any major newspaper today reveals horrors we are equally powerless to rationalize. Consider the case of Taliban "justice" in the Kabul Sports Stadium before a packed crowd in July 1998.[32] Ghulam Farooq, an apprentice ironworker, had been accused of theft.

> More than three years later, Farooq, 26, bowed his head to hold back tears as he described the final minutes before the silent doctor jabbed a hypodermic needle into his hand and put him to sleep. The mullahs already had finished their speeches about justice and the Koran and the will of God. The only sound Farooq remembers hearing as he drifted off were a few shouts from the stands.

"They were crying out to the Talibs not to do it, but they didn't care," he recalled last week.

When Farooq awoke about two hours later, he was in Kabul's Wazir Akbar Khan Hospital, minus his right hand and left foot. He was screaming in pain. The Taliban hung his severed hand and foot on lampposts as a warning to others.[33]

With Stott, I affirm that eternal conscious punishment strains our sense of justice. It weighs heavily on our emotions. But so does the daily news. Can anyone take it in? Can anyone make sense of things to the world's Ghulam Farooqs? To the bereaved of suicide bombers in Israel? To hapless victims of a Western serial killer? To any of their moms and dads?

I conclude that the difference between the woes of this world and of hell is only a matter of degree. I cannot make sense of any of it, and I am suspicious of anyone who says they can—anyone, that is, except Christ.

No one who has studied Jesus' words is a stranger to the experience of arriving at more and more unanswerable questions. One response to these questions is to allow the sensibilities of our age to redefine what his words mean. A second response is to take at his word the Savior who created the world and promises that he is even now redeeming it. If our best hope is Jesus, then our best counsel may be to receive his teachings, undiluted, in grave earnest.

# CHAPTER THREE

# THREE PICTURES OF HELL

## CHRISTOPHER W. MORGAN

EVERY NEW TESTAMENT AUTHOR writes about the coming future judgment or hell. Since the previous chapter covered Jesus' words, this chapter will briefly summarize what Paul, the author of Hebrews, James, Peter, Jude, and John each wrote about it. The focus here is threefold—to summarize the teaching on hell by each New Testament author, to show three predominant pictures of hell that emerge, and to provide some help in better understanding those pictures.

## HELL IN PAUL

Surprisingly, the word "hell" does not occur in Paul's writings. But Paul does teach about hell when he addresses the future punishment of unbelievers. It would take too much space to survey all that he writes, so we'll look only at Romans and 2 Thessalonians—Romans because it illustrates Paul's diverse handling of future punishment, and 2 Thessalonians because it contains Paul's most explicit and thorough teaching on the subject.[34]

## Romans

In his letter to the Roman church, Paul stresses the need to proclaim the gospel, which is God's way of bringing people to faith in Christ. Preaching the gospel is crucial because of the current sinful state of all humanity. Jews and Gentiles alike are under sin, under God's wrath, and will be judged. Only those who have faith in Christ will escape. In this portrayal of the predicament of sinners, Paul relates some important truths about the future punishment of the wicked.

1. Future punishment is connected to God's wrath. The wicked are presently under his wrath (1:18–32), are objects of wrath (9:22), continually store up wrath for the day of wrath (2:5–8; 3:5), and can be saved from wrath only by faith in Christ (5:9–21).

2. Future punishment is God's judgment. The wicked are deservedly condemned under the judgment of God, which is impartial, true, righteous, and certain (2:1–12; 3:7–8). This condemnation is the result of sin and is just punishment for sin (5:12–21; 6:23).

3. Future punishment will consist of "trouble and distress." This suffering shows no favoritism between Jews and Gentiles (2:8–11).

4. Future punishment consists of "death" and "destruction." Sinners deserve death (1:32), the wages of sin is death (6:16–23), as sinners we bear fruit for death (7:5), and those who live according to the flesh should expect death (8:13). Also, sinners are vessels of wrath "prepared for destruction" (9:22).

5. Both sin and future punishment are separation from Christ ("cursed and cut off from Christ" in 9:3).

## 2 Thessalonians

Paul teaches most directly about hell in 2 Thessalonians. As he encourages believers suffering persecution, Paul stresses that God's justice will prevail (1:5 – 10). In just a few verses, Paul emphasizes several important truths about hell.

1. Hell is the result of God's retributive justice on sinners ("God is just: He will pay back trouble to those who trouble you," 1:6).
2. Hell is punishment for those who do not know God and do not obey the gospel (1:8; 2:12).
3. Hell is eternal destruction (1:9; see also 2:3, 8, 10).
4. Hell is exclusion from Jesus' presence and majesty ("shut out from" in 1:9).

# HELL IN HEBREWS

Two passages in Hebrews talk about future judgment. Hebrews 6:1 – 3 refers to the future punishment of the wicked as "eternal judgment" (6:2), which the author says is an "elementary teaching" of the faith (cf. 6:1). Hebrews 10:27 – 30 depicts this judgment as fearful and dreadful, a "raging fire that will consume the enemies of God." It also teaches that hell comes from God as punishment, judgment, and retribution.

# HELL IN JAMES

The letter of James does not stress hell, though it does include some general statements about the future punishment of the wicked.[35]

1. Unbelievers are said to wither away and be destroyed (1:11).
2. Sin produces death as its offspring (1:15).
3. God is the Lawgiver and Judge who is able to both save and destroy sinners (4:12).
4. The wicked deserve to be punished severely, and this suffering is coming (5:1 – 5). To portray this suffering graphically,

James talks about "misery," "eating flesh with fire," and "the day of slaughter."

5. James concludes his letter by saying that sinners need to be turned from impending "death" (5:20).

## HELL IN PETER AND JUDE

Peter's second letter is filled with references to the future punishment of the wicked in hell, and Jude closely parallels 2 Peter 2. Peter and Jude both depict hell as "destruction" (2 Peter 2:1, 3, 12; Jude 5, 10, 11). Both liken hell to condemnation hanging over the wicked (2 Peter 2:3; Jude 4; the contextual reference is to false teachers). Hell is like a gloomy dungeon, where rebellious angels are held for judgment (2 Peter 2:4; Jude 6 is similar). Peter illustrates future punishment with the account of Sodom and Gomorrah's burning to ashes (2 Peter 2:6) and warns that God holds the unrighteous for the day of judgment while continuing their punishment (2:9). Peter also writes that hell is a place of retribution (2:13) and "blackest darkness" (2:17; Jude 13). Jude adds that hell is a punishment of eternal fire (Jude 7, 15, 23).

## HELL IN REVELATION

Written by John, Revelation contains some of the most noteworthy passages on hell in all of Scripture. Consider Revelation 14:9 – 11:

> If anyone worships the beast and its image and receives its mark on their forehead or on their hand, they, too, will drink the wine of God's fury, which has been poured full strength into the cup of his wrath. They will be tormented with burning sulfur in the presence of the holy angels and of the Lamb. And the smoke of their torment will rise for ever and ever. There will be no rest day or night for those who worship the beast and its image, or for anyone who receives the mark of its name.

Notice that hell in this passage is a place of intense suffering — even torment — where God's fury and wrath are felt at full force

(14:10). Hell is filled with "fire and sulfur" (14:10; see also a lake of "fire and sulfur" in 20:10, a "lake of fire" in 20:14–15, and a "lake that burns with fire and sulfur" in 21:8). It is a place where "the smoke of their torment rises for ever and ever" (14:11), and this torment is continual: "There will be no rest day or night" (14:11), and "they will be tormented day and night forever and ever" (20:10).

In another passage, Revelation 20:10–15, John emphasizes that hell is just punishment for the wicked. He also shows that God throws the devil, the beast, and the false prophet into hell. They do not rule or have any power there, but go to hell to receive their due punishment; they are not restored, but remain in hell to suffer forever.

The conclusion of Revelation is that God judges everyone— those whom the world deems important, those whom the world never notices, and everyone in between. John writes that "anyone whose name was not found written in the book of life was thrown into the lake of fire" (20:15). While God's people worship him in heaven forever, living in a state of perfect blessedness, sinners are banished from heaven, forever unable to enter in (see 20:14–15; 21:8). Sadly, they continue to exist outside of heaven—*after* God casts them into the lake of fire and *after* God makes all things new (21:5–8; 22:15).[36]

## THREE PREDOMINANT PICTURES OF HELL

Clearly, the future punishment of the wicked is a significant theme in the New Testament. Every New Testament author addresses it— that cannot be said of many other important biblical truths!

Yet this overview also shows that the New Testament teaching concerning hell is somewhat diverse. At times, the pictures of hell even seem irreconcilable. How can burning fire coexist with blackest darkness, for example? How can destruction be linked to continual, endless suffering? Instead of viewing these pictures as contradictory, however, we should understand them to be complementary. The different depictions of hell bring out shades of meaning that a single rendering could not.

Along these lines, it is interesting to note that each New Testament writer's descriptions do resemble the others, and sometimes, in fact, the diverse portraits of hell come from the same writer. Overall, three key depictions of hell recur with nearly every New Testament writer, and each depiction offers insight into the nature of eternal judgment.

## Punishment

The chief picture of hell is as a place of punishment, communicated by every single New Testament author. Three passages are most striking. In Matthew 25:31–46, Jesus claims the right as judge to consign the wicked to "eternal punishment" and to grant the righteous "eternal life." He concludes by forcefully contrasting the eternal destinies of the righteous and the wicked:

> Then he will say to those on his left, "Depart from me, you who are cursed, into the eternal fire prepared for the devil and his angels."... Then they will go away to eternal punishment, but the righteous to eternal life.

In 2 Thessalonians 1:5–10, a passage we looked at earlier, the apostle Paul encourages believers who are suffering persecution that "God is just: He will pay back trouble for those that trouble you.... He will punish those who do not know God and do not obey the gospel of our Lord Jesus. They will be punished with everlasting destruction."

As previously noted, Revelation 20:10–15 says that the wicked are cast into hell while the righteous experience the unhindered and glorious presence of God on the new earth.

From these and many other passages that describe hell as punishment, we learn the following:

1. The punishment is *deserved*. For clarity and emphasis, the biblical writers stress the justice of retributive punishment.
2. The punishment consists of *suffering*. Those in hell suffer intense and excruciating pain — emotional, spiritual, and

physical. Hell is worse than being drowned in the sea. It is worse than any earthly suffering, even being maimed. The suffering never ends. Those in hell will be thrown into the fiery furnace and will experience unimaginable sorrow, regret, remorse, and pain. The intensity of the suffering seems to be according to the wickedness of the person's behavior. And hell is utterly fearful and dreadful; the suffering is constant.

3. The punishment is *conscious*. If hell did not consist of conscious suffering, it is hard to see how it could be worse than death, worse than earthly suffering, filled with weeping and gnashing of teeth, or a place of misery. The biblical images show that people in hell will be aware of their suffering and just punishment.

4. The punishment is *eternal*. The never-ending nature of the punishment is shown vividly in Revelation 14:11, where it is said that the wicked "will have no rest day or night." The endlessness of the punishment is also confirmed by the forceful pronouncement in Revelation 20:10, "They will be tormented day and night for ever and ever."

## Destruction

Another prominent biblical picture of hell is one of destruction. Consider well-known passages such as John 3:16: "For God so loved the world that he gave his one and only Son, that whoever believes in him shall not *perish* but have eternal life" (emphasis added); and Romans 6:23: "For the wages of sin is *death*, but the gift of God is eternal life in Christ Jesus our Lord" (emphasis added). Both Revelation 20:14 and 21:8 also speak of hell as the "second death."

Some have pointed out that destruction can refer to utter annihilation, inferring that passages like the above describe the death of people in hell rather than their eternal conscious suffering. But destruction in the Bible can also imply loss, ruin, or corruption. New Testament scholar Douglas Moo has pointed out that when biblical authors speak of destruction, they often "refer to the situation of a person or object that has lost the essence of its nature or function."[37]

For instance, destruction in the Bible can refer to barren land (Ezek. 6:14), to ointment that is poured out wastefully (Mark 14:4), to wineskins with holes that no longer function (Matt. 9:17), to a lost coin (Luke 15:9), or even to the entire world that perished in the Flood (2 Peter 3:6). As Moo writes, "In none of these cases do the objects cease to exist; they cease to be useful or to exist in their original, intended state."[38]

Destruction is a graphic picture showing that those in hell have failed to embrace the meaning of life and have wasted it. Trying to find life in themselves and in sin, they forfeited true life. Only ruin and garbage remain.

## Banishment

The third central picture of hell is banishment. This idea of hell as separation or exclusion is especially prominent in the teachings of Jesus.

In the Sermon on the Mount, Jesus proclaims that he will judge the world and declare to unbelievers, "Away from me!" (Matt. 7:23), personally banishing them from his kingdom. Jesus also portrays hell as being outside God's kingdom and the wicked as being excluded from the kingdom. "Depart from me ... into the eternal fire prepared for the devil and his angels," Jesus says in his Mount of Olives sermon about the end times (25:41).

Whereas punishment stresses the active side of hell, banishment shows the horror of hell by highlighting what a person misses. Banishment is stronger than separation. It suggests God's active judgment, and it stresses the dreadfulness and finality of the predicament. The wicked never experience unhindered fellowship with God. They are forever kept from his majestic presence and completely miss out on the reason for their existence—to glorify and know their Creator.

Theologian Kendall Harmon suggests three aspects of hell associated with banishment: (1) Hell is being cut off from Christ and the kingdom of God. (2) Hell is God's judgment in giving over the sinner to himself (Rom. 1:24, 26, 28). (3) Hell is not being known by God (Luke 13:22–30).[39]

Addressing the banishment of the wicked from God and the glory of heaven, Augustine observed:

> To be lost out of the kingdom of God, to be an exile from the city of God, to be alienated from the life of God, to have no share in that great goodness which God has laid up for them that fear him, has wrought out for them that trust in him would be a punishment so great that, supposing it to be eternal, no torments that we know of, continued through as many ages as man's imagination can conceive, could be compared with it.[40]

## IMPORTANT CONSIDERATIONS ABOUT THE THREE PICTURES OF HELL

It is significant to note that the three pictures of hell are eternal and simultaneous: God's final sentence does not begin with banishment, continue with a period of punishment, and end with destruction, as some have suggested. Scripture offers no such order. Rather the three pictures offer multiple vantage points on a unified experience.

Much can be learned about hell by considering it as punishment. Other insights can be gleaned by viewing it as destruction. Further light can be shed on it by seeing it as banishment. The three pictures give more clarity and understanding than only one would. As Harmon writes:

> The crucial point is that the different images each refer to a single reality and that combining different images is not like putting together the pieces of a jigsaw puzzle, but rather like letting the sunlight reflect through a diamond and seeing each ray's colors as pointing towards a single eschatological truth.[41]

Furthermore, the three pictures of hell should be held in balance. Those who hold to the historic view of hell should not allow punishment alone to dominate their thoughts. Annihilationists err when they stretch the picture of destruction beyond what Scripture teaches. And most evangelicals need to guard against the tendency to view hell in passive terms like separation rather than banishment.

Finally, the three pictures of hell stand together and appear in the same passages. Jesus uses all of them in Matthew 24:45–25:46. The wicked servant is "cut into pieces"—destruction. He is assigned to a place with the hypocrites—banishment. And he suffers extreme pain in the punishment.

## IMPLICATIONS OF THE THREE PICTURES OF HELL

Admittedly, caution should be used when trying to understand how these three pictures of hell work together. But when studied carefully, side-by-side, they reveal several key implications that correspond with the overall biblical teaching on God, sin, the atonement, salvation, and heaven.

*The three pictures complement biblical portraits of God.* Hell as punishment vividly depicts God as the Judge who justly sentences the wicked. Hell as destruction portrays God as the Warrior or Victor who defeats his enemies. Hell as banishment views God as the King who allows only his citizens into his kingdom.

*The three pictures flow naturally from biblical portraits of sin.* Each picture of hell seems to be the logical result of an aspect of sin. Hell as punishment recognizes that sin is a crime. Hell as destruction sees that sin as spiritual death. Hell as banishment views sin as alienation from God.

Various pictures of hell also extend the present judgment of God on sin. God's wrath is on sinners, and hell is the culmination of that wrath. Sinners are condemned already, but they await their ultimate condemnation in hell. Sinners are now dead spiritually but await the second death. Unbelievers are alienated from God now but will be finally excluded from his presence. Sinners' hearts are dark now but will eternally be in "outer darkness" and "blackest darkness." The evidence is compelling: the pictures of hell can be viewed as culminations, extensions, intensifications, and logical continuations of the unbeliever's current state of sin.

It is also significant that the pictures of punishment, destruction, and banishment have Old Testament roots. They can be found as early as the fall recorded in Genesis 3, when God punished Adam and Eve with a curse, warned of sin's consequence of death, and banished them from the garden of Eden.

*The three pictures illustrate the biblical doctrine of the atonement.* On the cross, Jesus died as a substitute for our sins and drank the cup of wrath—punishment. On the cross, Jesus offers himself as a sacrifice for our sins—death. On the cross, Jesus experiences separation from the Father's fellowship as he cries, "My God, my God, why have you forsaken me?"—banishment.

*The three pictures stand in contrast to biblical portraits of salvation.* Hell as punishment awaits those who are not justified by faith. Hell as destruction awaits those who never receive new life in Christ. Hell as banishment is in store for all who have never been reconciled to God through Christ.

*Finally, the three pictures also contrast biblical portraits of the kingdom of heaven.* Hell as punishment stands opposite of heaven as a reward. Hell as destruction is the extreme counterpoint to heaven as eternal life. Hell as banishment stands in contrast with heaven as the kingdom and marvelous presence of God. Instead of inheriting the kingdom in Christ, unbelievers are punished eternally.

# CHAPTER FOUR

# THREE PERSPECTIVES ON HELL

## ROBERT A. PETERSON

CONSIDER THREE DIFFERENT vantage points on a classic baseball series, the 2003 National League championship between the Chicago Cubs and the Florida Marlins. Some Chicago fans, devoted to their Cubbies, wept openly as the last out of the seventh game secured the series for the Marlins. Marlins fans, however, celebrated as their heroes posted a second improbable victory, the first being over the San Francisco Giants, and headed for a World Series confrontation with the New York Yankees. "Neutral" baseball watchers like me, who were devoted to neither the Cubs nor the Marlins, merely enjoyed an exciting series without the strong pull of partisan emotions.

The biblical doctrine of hell can also be looked at from many vantage points. This chapter will explore three often-neglected ones, namely: (1) the Trinity, (2) divine sovereignty and human freedom, and (3) fulfilled and not-yet-fulfilled teaching of the last things.

# HELL FROM THE VANTAGE POINT OF THE TRINITY

Many who reject the old caricature of the angry God of the Old Testament and the loving Jesus of the New nevertheless view judgment as the work of the Father. The Son, it is assumed, is the Savior, not the Judge. The Holy Spirit is usually not brought into the picture at all.

This picture is distorted. While the Son is indeed Savior of the world, according to more than a dozen passages of Scripture he is also the Judge. In addition, the unity of the Godhead demands that we also see the Holy Spirit at work in judgment. Only by viewing the last judgment from a Trinitarian perspective will we gain a proper vision.

Numerous passages teach that God the Father is Judge. It is the "Father who judges each person's work impartially" (1 Peter 1:17). The Father, portrayed as sitting on "a great white throne" of Judgment, is the One from whose presence "the earth and the heavens fled" (Rev. 20:11). And the Father is depicted as the divine host from whom the wicked "will drink the wine of God's fury, which has been poured full strength into the cup of his wrath" (Rev. 14:10).

The Son too is Judge. The Gospels ascribe judgment to "the Son of Man," who "is going to come in his Father's glory with his angels, and then will reward each person according to what they have done" (Matt. 16:27). In Matthew 25, the returning King Jesus sits on his throne with all humankind gathered before him. He separates the people of the world, sending them to one of two destinies: "eternal punishment" or "eternal life." "Depart from me, you who are cursed," he says, "into the eternal fire prepared for the devil and his angels" (25:41).

In the Gospels Jesus also is Judge of unclean spirits. "What do you want with me, Jesus, Son of the Most High God?" an evil spirit asks him in Mark 5:6. "In God's name don't torture me!"

Though Jesus says in John 5 that he did not come to condemn

sinners but to save them, he also says: "Moreover, the Father judges no one, but has entrusted all judgment to the Son, that all may honor the Son just as they honor the Father" (5:22). Those who reject Jesus as Savior will one day face him as Judge, and when he judges, he will confirm that he too is God.

In the book of Acts, Peter tells the Athenians at the meeting of the Areopagus that God "has set a day when he will judge the world with justice by the man he has appointed. He has given proof of this to everyone by raising him from the dead" (Acts 17:31). The apostle Paul reveals more specifics about Jesus' judgment in 2 Thessalonians 1:

> This will happen when the Lord Jesus is revealed from heaven in blazing fire with his powerful angels. He will punish those who do not know God and do not obey the gospel of our Lord Jesus. They will be punished with everlasting destruction and shut out from the presence of the Lord, and from the glory of his might on the day he comes to be glorified in his holy people and to be marveled at among all those who have believed (2 Thess. 1:7–10).

Finally, in Revelation, Jesus the Lamb is alone qualified to open the seals of judgment. When he opens the sixth seal, the wicked cry out, "Fall on us and hide us from the face of him who sits on the throne and from the wrath of the Lamb! For the great day of their wrath has come, and who can withstand it?" (Rev. 6:16–17).

All throughout the New Testament we see Christ as both Savior and Judge—and we see the Father and the Son working together in judgment. That's why the doctrine of judgment cannot be properly understood apart from a Trinitarian context. The Father is the Judge who sends unrepentant sinners to hell—and so is the Son.

Please understand, however, that I am not presenting salvation and judgment as equals. God delights to save people from their sins; he takes no delight in the death of the wicked. Likewise Jesus came into the world in order to save it. But the Bible is clear that not all people will believe in him. As a result, it repeats over and over that Jesus and the Father will one day judge.

What about the Holy Spirit? His role in judgment is never clearly spelled out, but Jesus hints at his participation in some of his last words to the disciples: "When he [the Holy Spirit] comes, he will prove the world to be in the wrong about sin and righteousness and judgment" (John 16:8).

Overall, remembering that the Godhead works in unity in judgment will keep us from pitting one member against another. It will also keep us from certain misunderstandings and controversies about hell.

# HELL FROM THE VANTAGE POINT OF DIVINE SOVEREIGNTY AND HUMAN FREEDOM

One of the most helpful tensions in the Bible is between God's sovereignty and human freedom. Simply put: Does God determine the events of a person's life, or do persons themselves? The Bible regularly joins these opposite notions as if they worked together rather than contradict each other, in order to provide us with a fuller view of reality.

I will look at two biblical examples of this tension, and then show how it can help us to better understand hell.

## Joseph's Being Sold into Slavery

Genesis records one of the cruelest betrayals in the Bible: Joseph's brothers selling him into slavery. The brothers were offended by Joseph's dreams and sold him to Ishmaelite merchants. The merchants then sold him to an Egyptian named Potiphar, and eventually, through a series of unlikely events, Joseph rose to the position of second-in-command over all Egypt. While Joseph was in that position his brothers came to Egypt to buy food from him because of the severe worldwide famine. They did not recognize him, but Joseph's words shocked them:

> I am your brother Joseph, the one you sold into Egypt! And now, do not be distressed and do not be angry with yourselves for selling me here, because it was to save lives that God sent me ahead of you.... So, then, it was not you who sent me here, but God. (Gen. 45:4–5, 8)

As readers, we want to protest, "Of course Joseph's brothers sent him to Egypt!" But Joseph is not denying that fact; he just said that they had sold him into Egypt. Rather, he is appealing to a higher cause for his journey to Egypt—God's sovereign hand. Scripture here teaches that the same event had both a human and a divine cause. Joseph's brothers sent him into Egypt and so did God. Their sin and God's plan were carried out by the same deed.

This mysterious truth is demonstrated throughout Scripture, but we must be careful how we understand it. God's sovereign control does not turn the brothers' sin into something good, nor does it implicate God in their sin. They sinned against God and their brother when they sold him into slavery. However, neither does the brothers' sin frustrate God's plan.

After their father Jacob dies, Joseph's brothers fear for their lives, reasoning that Joseph may take revenge now that their father is gone. His response overflows with grace—and an understanding of the tension between God's sovereignty and human freedom. "Don't be afraid. Am I in the place of God? You intended to harm me, but God intended it for good.... So then, don't be afraid" (Gen. 50:19–21).

Here Scripture teaches that the same event can even have two different motives. The brothers intended harm but God intended good. God is, therefore, not chargeable with the harm, though he deserves credit for the good that he brought out of it.

## Christ's Betrayal and Crucifixion

This mystery of God's sovereignty and human freedom is nowhere more evident than in the crucifixion of Christ. Notice how Jesus speaks of Judas's betrayal: "The Son of Man will go as it has been decreed, but woe to that man who betrays him" (Luke 22:22). Jesus submits to God's plan when he utters these words. At the same time, however, he holds his betrayer, Judas Iscariot, culpable.

Does Judas's betrayal of Jesus make it necessary for God to adjust his plan? Not at all. Listen to the apostle Peter's words:

> This man was handed over to you by God's deliberate plan and foreknowledge.
>
> Indeed Herod and Pontius Pilate met together with the Gentiles and the people of Israel in this city to conspire against your holy servant Jesus, whom you anointed. They did what your power and will had decided beforehand should happen. (Acts 2:23; 4:27–28).

Note that when sinners did the worst they could against Jesus, they only did what God had already decided would happen. Other Scriptures say that Jesus' saving death was included in God's plan before creation. It was certain that Jesus would be crucified.

At the same time, Jesus' crucifixion was the greatest injustice ever perpetrated. The tension between God's sovereignty and human freedom is indeed mysterious. To tamper with either produces terrible misunderstandings. To deny human responsibility, for instance, transforms the conspirators against Jesus into God's servants who do good when they crucify Jesus. To minimize divine sovereignty transforms the cross into an emergency measure of God. Both transformations are wrong in the extreme.

## Hell, God's Sovereignty, and Human Freedom

The tension between God's sovereignty and humanity's freedom is also evident in God's sending of guilty sinners to hell.

God's sovereignty is expressed in his judgment. This theme recurs a number of times in the Gospels and Revelation, and it shows that the power of God over the wicked extends beyond the grave. The Bible also indicates that God rules over hell. Unfortunately, some have erred at this point. As one writer said, "Hell is where Satan rules ... where his complete fury is unleashed."[42] But this is wrong, for hell is where God alone rules and where his fury is unleashed against Satan, his angels, and wicked human beings.

The book of Revelation also says that God chooses who will go to heaven—in fact, that he has enrolled their names "in the book of life from the creation of the world" (Rev. 17:8).

A focus on God's sovereignty doesn't tell the whole story, however. Throughout the Bible, eternal judgment is most often traced to misused human freedom. Both the Old and New Testaments say that God will judge sinners according to their deeds:

> I will deal with them according to their conduct, and by their own standards I will judge them. Then they will know that I am the LORD. (Ezek. 7:27)

> The LORD Almighty has done to us what our ways and practices deserve, just as he determined to do. (Zech. 1:6)

> For the Son of Man is going to come ... and then he will reward each person according to what they have done. (Matt. 16:27)

> Do not be deceived: God cannot be mocked. A man reaps what he sows. The one who sows to please his sinful nature, from that nature will reap destruction. (Gal. 6:7–8)

Passage after passage points to a just God who gives sinners what they deserve. Those whose lives are characterized by evil thoughts, words, and deeds reap God's wrath. Why do people end up in hell? Scripture repeatedly blames human freedom used wrongly.

Revelation 20 captures both sides of the picture, showing how God's sovereignty and human freedom work together in determining who will go to hell.

> Then I saw a great white throne and him who was seated on it. The earth and the heavens fled from his presence, and there was no place for them. And I saw the dead, great and small, standing before the throne, and books were opened. Another book was opened, which is the book of life. The dead were judged according to what they had done as recorded in the books. The sea gave up the dead that were in it, and death and Hades gave up the dead that were in them, and each person was judged according to what they had done. Then death and Hades were thrown into the lake of fire. The lake of fire is the second death. Anyone whose name was not found written in the book of life was thrown into the lake of fire. (Rev. 20:11–15)

Summing it all up, Scripture presents God as the sovereign Judge before whom sinners stand on judgment day. They are condemned for abusing their human freedom in their rebellion against their Maker.

If we press Scripture further, we see that God has sovereignly chosen multitudes for salvation before the creation of the world and has passed over others, allowing them to reap punishment for their sins. With Scripture we confess that God stands behind the destiny of every human being. But with Scripture we also confess that he does so differently with the saved and the unsaved. He is proactive in saving; he grants grace to those who would perish without it. But he is passive in judging, allowing sinners to receive what their sins deserve.

Although we cannot fully explain this mystery, we confess its truth, even as we confess the mysteries of the Trinity and the fully human and fully divine natures of Jesus.

## HELL FROM THE VANTAGE POINT OF FULFILLED AND NOT-YET-FULFILLED TEACHING OF THE LAST THINGS

One of the most important observations about biblical prophecy is that some parts have already been fulfilled while others have not. This is often called the "already" and "not yet" of prophecy. The "already" refers to the greatest event predicted in the Old Testament, the coming of the Messiah. The "not yet" refers to Jesus' second coming and the end times.

While there are roots to this "already/not yet" aspect of God's plan in the Old Testament, it is more fully seen in the New Testament. Many New Testament teachings are affected by it, including signs of the end of the world, our adoption as God's children, the coming of the Antichrist, and more. Thus, while salvation and judgment belong mostly to the last day—they are "not yet" fulfilled— they can also be seen in the present—they are "already" here.

As beautifully as anywhere in Scripture, 1 John 3:1–3 combines the realized and unrealized aspects of salvation:

> See what great love the Father has lavished on us, that we should be called children of God! And that is what we are!... Dear friends, now we are children of God, and what we will be has not yet been made known. But we know that when Christ appears, we shall be like him, for we shall see him as he is. All who have this hope in him purify themselves, just as he is pure.

John knows that "now we are children of God," but he also writes "what we will be has not yet been made known."

Judgment, too, is partly fulfilled and partly unfulfilled. We see the "already" aspect in the verses immediately following John 3:16:

> For God did not send his Son into the world to condemn the world, but to save the world through him. Whoever believes in him is not condemned, but whoever does not believe stands condemned already because he has not believed in the name of God's one and only Son. (John 3:17–18)

For every believer in Christ the verdict of the last day is announced ahead of time—he or she is "not condemned." Similarly, for everyone who rejects the Son the final verdict is also already announced—he or she is "condemned already."

Yet it is incorrect to say that heaven and hell are merely what one makes of this life, because Scripture's main focus when speaking of both is on what lies ahead.

Here is what will happen. Christ will return in glory. As Matthew writes, "When the Son of Man comes in his glory, and all the angels with him, he will sit on his glorious throne" (Matt. 25:31). At his word all of the dead will rise: "... all who are in their graves will hear his voice and come out" (John 5:28–29). Then, he will make the final separation between the saved and unsaved. Indeed, "all the nations will be gathered before him, and he will separate the people one from another as a shepherd separates the sheep from the goats"

(Matt. 25:32). King Jesus will invite God's children to enter into their inheritance but will banish unbelievers "into the eternal fire prepared for the devil and his angels" (Matt. 25:34, 41).

As succinctly as any verse in Scripture, Matthew 25:46 describes the final destinies of the lost and saved: "Then they will go away to eternal punishment, but the righteous to eternal life."

To summarize: Judgment, like salvation, is "already" and "not yet." Already believers are justified before God and unbelievers are condemned. At Christ's return, the dead will be resurrected — the righteous for eternal bliss and the wicked for eternal punishment. These truths should drive unsaved persons to Christ for eternal life. They should drive those who know the Lord to love and pray for unsaved persons and to speak with them about their eternal destinies.

# CHAPTER FIVE

# DOES EVERY-ONE GO TO HEAVEN?

## J. I. PACKER

A CHRISTIAN UNIVERSALIST is someone who believes that every human being will finally come to enjoy everlasting salvation. Among competing worldviews, it appears as an extreme optimism about the future. Each and every one of us, it declares, and all of us together, will end up in a state of supreme God-given bliss.

Universalism is a challenge to Christian orthodoxy, whether Roman Catholic, Eastern Orthodox, or Protestant evangelical, for the church has officially declared universalism a heresy since the second Council of Constantinople in AD 553. In recent years, however, universalism has made something of a comeback.

Applied to our six-billion-person, global-village world — multicultural, multifaith, and endlessly diverse as it is — the scope of universalism is breathtaking. It covers all the dead from earliest times as well as all the living, both present and future. It embraces all the adherents of all the religions and cults that ever have been or shall be. It extends to the many millions who have no interest in religion.

Bloody-handed practitioners of treachery, genocide, and torture, as well as bloody-minded devotees of personal cruelty and child abuse are included. No one is left out.

In the end, universalism represents a kind of paternalism in which each person is assured that whatever final destiny they anticipate, hopefully or fearfully, and whatever their present pattern of life, religious or not, moral or not, the Christian's Christ-centered salvation will be theirs—whether or not they want such a salvation.

## THE CASE FOR UNIVERSALISM

Most universalists, though not all, concede that universalism is not clearly taught in the Bible. What, then, is the warrant for it? The deepest motivation for universalism has always been a revolt against the endless punishment of the unsaved. Universalists often argue that God in his love wants to reconcile all to himself, and that sooner or later God must achieve his purpose. Madeleine L'Engle, the gifted Christian fantasy novelist, puts it like this:

> I know a number of highly sensitive and intelligent people in my own communion [i.e., Anglicanism] who consider as a heresy my faith that God's loving concern for his creation will outlast all our willfulness and pride. No matter how many eons it takes, he will not rest until all of creation, including Satan, is reconciled to him, until there is no creature who cannot return his look of love with a joyful response of love.... I cannot believe that God wants punishment to go on interminably any more than does a loving parent. The entire purpose of loving punishment is to teach, and it lasts only as long as is needed for the lesson. And the lesson is always love.[43]

Rejecting an endless hell is prompted partly by compassion for one's fellow humans, but mainly by the thought that inflicting eternal punishment is unworthy of God, since it would negate his love.

Motivationally, then, universalists agree, but not in theology. Far from it! On closer inspection, universalism dissolves into a cluster of distinct positions.

Some present universal salvation as a certainty; others, such as the Swiss theologian Karl Barth, embrace it simply as a pious hope.[44] Some envisage it as the fruit of postmortem evangelism. Others predict a chastening experience for some in hell, though hell is guaranteed to end up empty.

Most universalists have affirmed that all will eventually acknowledge Christ as Lord (see Phil. 2:9 – 11). They will praise and adore him, fellowship with him, and find their salvation and joy in so doing. However, some have based this confidence in their belief that God is sovereign in calling people to himself. Others have rooted it in a glowing vision — a somewhat incoherent vision, it must be said — of God persuasively wearing down free human agents until, in some sense against their will, unbelievers bow to his will. Still others base their universalism on the idea that all religions are essentially the same.

What our survey, by no means exhaustive, points to is the fact that (1) the various universalisms are spinoffs of other beliefs about God, and (2) universalism in all its forms is a human wish seeking a divine warrant. What holds universalists together is a shared sense of embarrassment, indeed outrage, at the thought of a loving God excluding anyone from final happiness.

There are several reasons why universalism is making strides today. First, living in multireligious communities and rubbing shoulders regularly with people of many faiths, we would like to be able to tell ourselves that their religions are as good for them as ours is for us. Whatever salvation is, we want to hope it will finally be both theirs and ours.

Second, few today are clear on the specifics of the Christian way of salvation and on how it differs from what is hoped for in Hinduism, Buddhism, Islam, and other world faiths. Little problem is seen in treating all religions as one, and thus universalism is taken for granted.

Third, with Christianity losing ground so fast in the West, it is reassuring to think that God will save all those who now shrug off Christianity as an irrelevance. Reassurance in the face of troubling facts is always welcome.

Finally, establishing rapport with non-Christians remains important for many of us, and universalism naturally fits this end. For this reason it seems likely that universalism, which has already come to stay, will generate more interest in the future than it does now.

In any case, we must face up to the two far-reaching claims that all forms of universalism make. The first claim is that universalism alone does justice to the love of God revealed in the Bible—and to the victory of Jesus Christ the Savior over sin and death. While sitting loosely on some biblical teachings, universalists insist that the overall trajectory of the Bible fits their view. By contrast, they claim, any belief in unending torment makes God a failure and something of a devil. This is a bold claim, implying that most Christians' belief in hell has grossly dishonored God.

The second claim, which is not always verbalized but is constantly implicit, is that evangelism is not the prime task of Christian mission. In 1979 the Faith and Order Commission of the World Council of Churches redefined Christian mission to focus on the social, political, and economic well-being of the nations, with evangelism and church planting added in if circumstances allowed. Had I been a universalist, I should have taken in stride this politicized adjustment of Christian missionary priorities, for I would have realized that if all are "Doomed to be Saved," as the title of a nineteenth-century tract put it, then evangelizing may be less urgent. Other ways of loving my neighbor could take priority over seeking to win him or her to Christ.

Indeed, for more than a century a humanitarian agenda and universalist inclinations have frequently gone together. Even many nonuniversalist pastors seem to think similarly; they teach and practice goodwill as if everyone is heading for heaven and no danger of eternal hell exists.

## ASSESSING UNIVERSALISM

We must test universalism against the teaching of the Bible, and because the Bible has been pressed into service in various ways by universalists, it will be helpful to state how the Bible ought to be used.

In most versions of universalist thinking, biblical teaching is taken to be true and trustworthy; biblical interpretation and application are singled out as the areas of dispute. Now the proper principles of interpretation are, and always will be, that it must be context-specific, author-specific, and focus-specific.

That means, first, that passages must be interpreted in terms of the flow of thought of which they are a part. Their meaning should not be extrapolated beyond the limits of this flow of thought; otherwise, we will be reading into them what cannot truly be read out of them.

It also means that writers must be assumed not to contradict themselves. They must be respected as knowing their own minds. Thus, what they write in one place must be treated as coherent with what they write elsewhere.

Finally, it means that in seeking the writer's meaning, we must never lose sight of the immediate point he is making and the effect that he says he wants to produce in his readers. The way into the mind, meaning, and message of God in the Bible is always through the mind, meaning, and message of its human writers. Though many passages in the Bible carry a greater weight of meaning than their divinely led human writers knew, none carries less meaning. None should ever be treated as if these three guidelines do not apply to it.

Therefore, any impressionistic selectivity that discounts some things Scripture says while claiming to detect and affirm the Bible's general thrust on a given topic—as if the Bible were out of sync with itself—is a false trail. To follow any such trail is a mistake of mental method.

One caution, however: We must remember that all the things the Bible says about God involve what is called *analogical* language. That is, the meaning of words about God must be adjusted from the meaning of those words when used about humans.

Why must this adjusting be done? Because of the many ways in which God differs from humans. Since God made us in his own image and likeness, words about us can be used of him and vice versa. However, we are finite and sinful, while God is neither. So adjustments are needed to drop any implications of imperfection in our words about God. The Bible's authors consistently call for these kinds of adjustments. As Oxford professor Basil Mitchell explained:

> That God is [spirit] dictates that "father" does not mean "physical progenitor," but the word continues to bear the connotation of tender protective care. Similarly God's "wisdom" ... [does] not, for example, have to be learned, since he is omniscient and eternal.[45]

When the Bible speaks of God's "wrath" against persons who sin, for instance—or says that God "loves," "hates," or "repents"—we must remember that the words are analogical and should be interpreted within the rest of what the Bible says about God. Otherwise, we will lapse into false inferences—such as when some say that a good father would never expose his son to the suffering Jesus underwent on the cross, or that the cross was child abuse, or that God's repenting shows he did not foresee the consequences of his actions.[46]

The relevance of all this to hell will appear shortly. At present, suffice it to say that in assessing universalism we will seek only to read in Scripture what is really there, letting the inspired writers show us what they meant and construing the analogical aspects of the Bible's teaching appropriately.

## THE MEANING OF SALVATION

When universalists affirm the salvation of all, they clearly are talking about salvation in its full Christian sense. So let us remind ourselves of what that is. Salvation, in Scripture as in life, is being rescued from jeopardy and misery, preserved and kept safe from evil and disaster, protected against hostile forces, and firmly established in a state of security. The Bible focuses throughout on God as the One who saves and on needy humans as beneficiaries of his saving action.

Thus, we read of God's saving Israel from Egyptian captivity, Jonah from the fish's belly, the psalmist from death, and so on. But the master theme of the New Testament is God's gift of eternal salvation through Jesus Christ the Lord. By this gift, guilty and help-less humans are delivered from sin, God's wrath, death, and hell.

Christian salvation has three tenses—past, present, and future. Believers have been saved from sin's *penalty*, are being saved from its *power*, and will one day be saved from its *presence*, for there will be no sin in heaven. At each stage, salvation centers on a personal relation-ship with Jesus, a relationship marked by faith and love.

Do universalists really understand salvation in these terms, how-ever? To answer this question, we must look at three different kinds of salvation that universalists propose. I'll call them secular salvation, postmortem salvation, and pluralist salvation.

*Secular salvation* holds that everyone dies into some sort of hap-piness. No knowledge of God or relationship with Jesus is needed, either before or after death. Because this vision of salvation leaves out any communion with the Father and the Son by the Spirit, it is appropriate to call it secular—and we can safely strike it from consideration as a biblical alternative.

*Postmortem salvation* imagines that after death God will evange-lize all who left this world without faith in Jesus. He will confront them with their sin and introduce them to Jesus, and he will con-tinue to do this until they turn to Jesus in repentance and faith. How exactly God will bring this about is variously explained, and the speculations raise problems, as we will see. But for the moment it is enough to notice that, in contrast to the secular vision of salva-tion, postmortem salvation works with a fully Christian picture of salvation.

By contrast, *pluralist salvation* is deeply problematical. It holds that a wide range of religious thoughts, beliefs, convictions, and points of view are good, because all have validity and enrich each other. Instead of contrasting them, the pluralist seeks to blend them as fully as possible.

As one of the noteworthy adherents of pluralism, John Hick, has written, pluralism involves "rejecting the premise that God has revealed himself in any unique or definitive sense in Jesus Christ ...

[Jesus] is simply one of many great religious leaders who have been used by God to provide salvation for humankind."[47] All authentic religions, says Hick, diagnose the human condition as imperfect and offer a path via their teaching to salvation and fulfillment.[48] The differences between Christianity and other faiths are simply surface variations.

We need not follow pluralist speculations further. Clearly, pluralism does not affirm, nor can it affirm, Christian salvation in which all the redeemed find their ultimate delight in worshiping Jesus.

However, a distinction does need to be drawn here between the pluralist and the inclusivist. An inclusivist might speculate that good pagans — those leaving this world in a spirit of humble trust in an unknown God — are in possession of a saving relationship with God, though they do not realize it. Inclusivists do not know how after death such people will come to a full knowledge of God, but they are sure they will. Two different visions of salvation are at work between the pluralist and the inclusivist, and they must not be confused.

## THE MEANING OF ETERNAL PUNISHMENT

Our survey of universalist ideas about salvation has shown the speculative nature of all of them. It has also uncovered one of the motives that drives universalism today, namely, a desire to affirm all major religions as highways to the highest human happiness, so that no adherent of a different faith need ever convert to Christianity. Evident here may be a wish to explode the accusation, widespread in Hinduism and Islam, that Christianity is religious imperialism from the arrogant West.

We did not dwell on how all universalist attitudes negate the Christian mission as defined by Jesus and modeled by the apostles and the early church, though we might have done so with more space. All we did was note that fanciful ideas about salvation enter into every form of universalism, setting aside those versions that clearly lead to unbiblical thinking.

Now we will focus on another main aspect of universalism: the belief that a good God would never allow agony without end to be anyone's final destiny. What does the Bible say about eternal punishment?

To begin with, the phrase "eternal punishment" can be found in Jesus' parable about the sheep and the goats (Matt. 25:31–46). In this parable, Jesus speaks of himself as the Son of Man who executes the purpose of "my Father." Part of this purpose is judging "all the nations," separating those who will inherit God's kingdom from those who will be banished to "the eternal fire prepared for the devil and his angels."

The lesson is that one's faith is validated by the quality of one's life. So the wicked "go away to eternal punishment, but the righteous to eternal life." "Eternal" means belonging to the age to come, which in contrast to the present world will not end. "Punishment" means retributive pain inflicted by the one whose authority has been flouted.

According to O. C. Quick, an early twentieth-century professor of theology at Oxford, Matthew 25 is one of the two most explicit New Testament passages that affirm permanent and painful punishment for some after death. Quick's other passage is Revelation 20, where those whose names are not in the book of life are thrown into a lake of fire "for ever and ever." Quick observed that the anti-universalist teaching in the New Testament was "conclusive."[49]

Eternal punishment is not merely a matter of these two texts, however. Jesus said, "Anyone who speaks against the Holy Spirit will not be forgiven, either in this age or in the age to come" (Matt. 12:32). He also said it was better to get rid of a hand, foot, or eye that triggers sin than "to be thrown into hell 'where the worms that eat them do not die and the fire is not quenched'" (Mark 9:43–48). In his teaching on neighborly love, Jesus envisages a hardhearted rich man describing his after-death state as "agony in this fire" (Luke 16:24). Cries of agony and gnashing of teeth in outer darkness and a fiery furnace also appear in Jesus' other teachings.

One can see why the nineteenth-century Presbyterian theologian W. G. T. Shedd wrote: "Jesus Christ is the person who is responsible for the doctrine of eternal perdition [hell]."[50] Indeed he is.

As an earlier chapter in this book has shown, every New Testament author mentions hell as well. Anyone who thinks these passages are inconclusive must answer the question: How could our Lord and his apostles have been any clearer? What more could they have said to put everyone out of doubt about their meaning? To recognize the reality of eternal punishment is, to be sure, awesome, jolting, and traumatic, but surely there is no room for confusion that this was exactly what Jesus and his apostles wanted their hearers to recognize.

Furthermore, the theory of annihilationism, in which unbelievers are not tortured but destroyed in hell, must be read into the Bible. It cannot be read out of it, since the fire of hell in the Bible is a picture not of destruction but of ongoing pain, as Luke 16:24 makes unambiguously clear. Also, those who seek to explain away hell in order to safeguard God's moral praiseworthiness fail to see that New Testament authors saw hell not as creating a moral problem but as resolving one — namely, the problem of rebellious evil and human cruelty being allowed to run loose in God's world. Joy flows, and will forever flow, from the knowledge that God will finally exercise righteous judgment (Rom. 2:5).

So the task for the universalist is to circumvent the seemingly clear New Testament teaching on eternal punishment. Today's universalists for the most part posit that the unconverted will spend time in hell exposed to postmortem evangelism, along with steady divine pressure on their spirits, until the moment comes when they emerge, transformed, to join in the ongoing praises of the Lamb. Hell thus becomes, in the words of theologian Emil Brunner, "a pedagogic cleansing process."[51]

Nels Ferré was the most exuberant expositor of this line of thought in the twentieth century. He stated that love for enemies is part of God's character, so "if eternal hell is real, love is eternally frustrated and heaven is a place of mourning and concern for the lost." He went on to write:

> There may be many hells. There may be enough freedom even in the life of hell for man to keep rejecting God for a very long time. Hell may be not only unto the end of the age, but also unto the end of several ages. It cannot be eternal, but it can be longer than we think, depending upon the depth and stubbornness of our actual freedom now and whether or not God will give us fuller freedom in the life to come, and how much.[52]

However, Ferré notes, "God has no permanent problem children," and in hell he will "put on the screws tighter and tighter until we come to ourselves and are willing to consider the good he has prepared for us."[53]

This is typical universalist thinking, in which hell becomes not eternal punishment but a place of God's grace. It is a rough place, a house of correction and conversion, the means by which the perverse and deluded come to their senses.

How do the universalists justify their hypothesis? If you will pardon this long list of verses you can look up later, they point to three groups of passages: six allegedly predicting the salvation of all (John 12:32; Acts 3:21; Rom. 5:18; 11:32; 1 Cor. 15:22–28; Phil. 2:9–11); two supposedly announcing God's intention to save all (1 Tim. 2:4; 2 Peter 3:9); and five held to affirm that through Christ's death on the cross, God must and will eventually save all (2 Cor. 5:19; Gal. 1:20; Titus 2:11; Heb. 2:9; 1 John 2:2). They argue that everything the Bible teaches about eternal punishment must be read in light of these verses.

But their argumentation is, to say the least, forlorn. First, the contexts of the passages above are all either limited or generalized so that it is impossible to say they refer to every human being everywhere, past, present, and future, being destined for salvation. Most commentaries see in these passages only that God will save his people and restore his world, and that the invitation of the gospel applies to everyone to whom it comes. What universalists read into the texts cannot be read out of them.

Second, all but one of the New Testament books quoted above by universalists also contain statements about the final destruction of some because of their unbelief. Unless we assume that the biblical writers did not know their own minds, we must conclude that they did not contradict themselves and cannot have meant to affirm universal salvation.

Third, it must be said strongly that there is no biblical support for any form of postmortem evangelism. What appears instead is a drumbeat insistence on the decisiveness of this life's decisions. As long ago as 1908, Robert Mackintosh, himself a universalist, wrote: "The question is generally argued as one of New Testament interpretation, but the present writer does not think that hopeful. He sees no ground for challenging the old doctrine on exegetical [biblical] lines."[54]

We should also note that universalist speculation about eternal punishment is more than a little incoherent. The basic assertion is that God in love purposes everyone's salvation. But how can that be if, as most universalists believe, human freedom excludes divine control? If God so limited his power that he could not convert all in this world, however much he wanted to, then how can we be sure he will be able to do it hereafter?

From all standpoints, then, the universalist theorizing about eternal punishment must be judged unsuccessful. It is highly speculative and wholly out of line with what the Bible actually teaches.

## THE MEANING OF THE LOVE OF GOD

The famous liberal theologian Friedrich Schleiermacher argued "that if eternal damnation existed, eternal bliss could not, since the awareness of those suffering in hell would ruin the blessedness of those in heaven."[55] Many believe that universalism grasps God's loving character better than the traditional doctrine of hell. God's character is thus for universalists the true central battlefield.

How is the biblical truth about God's love to be ascertained? "Love" is a much-abused word in our culture, having been cheapened to mean liking things for oneself or indulging particular people ("I love my son so I give him everything he wants"). The Bible's presentation of God's love for his creatures is, however, quite different.

In Scripture, God's love is framed by three realities. The first is his ownership of, and rule over, all that he has made—that is, *his universal lordship*. He is always on the throne and in control. Second is *his holiness*, whereby he requires virtue of us, recoils from our vices, and judges the rebellious for what they have done. The third reality is *everybody's actual sinfulness*. It is within this framework that God's love finds expression. It is always extended as mercy from the holy Lord to persons who do not deserve any good gift from his hand.

Thus, God's love can never be seen as merited. Though it embraces vast numbers of people simultaneously, it also focuses personally on every individual it benefits. God loves all members of the human family in some ways (see Ps. 145:9) and out of these he draws some, spiritually dead though they are, to trust and new life in Christ.

What is God's revealed plan of love? It is a plan to restore a fallen world. The entire human race is guilty and corrupt, but God has chosen to create a new humanity through Jesus. For this he has chosen and called to faith people from every tribe and language and people and nation. Such is God's strategy of love. That this plan contains elements of mystery—that is, divine facts beyond our full understanding—is not a new discovery. The question "Why has God chosen to show his sovereign mercy in saving this sinner and not that one?" goes back to the early church and probably to the apostle Paul (see Rom. 9). We cannot know the answer. Indeed, our part is not to figure it out but to invite others, as Jesus and the apostles did, to turn to Jesus and enter new life.

Because everyone, including ourselves, deserves eternal punishment in hell, the supreme mystery is that God should save anyone. It is a wonder. Knowing these things must keep God's people in endless praise, both here and hereafter.

The universalists' idea of God's love, however, is progressive rather than restorative. In essence, universalists reason that God owes it—if not to sinful humans, at least to himself—to make sure that all souls without exception should eventually come to share in the life of love and joy that his people already enjoy. God does not save some from among others; all will finally be saved by Jesus. The controlling image is of a kind of therapy, in which God uses hell to restore to health those apart from him. This idea is compassionate, but it is also unbiblical and unrealistic.

Universalists seem not to understand sin. Leaving Scripture behind, they second-guess God's plan by contending that he uses hell to get sinners back on track at last. In so doing they fail to take the full measure of the tragic twisting and shattering brought about by sin. Their account of God's love seems shallow compared to God's love in the Bible.

Typically, universalists think God created our free will, giving us dignity and final determination over our choices. They do not see that, in the addictive grip of sin, choosing salvation is an impossibility. There is a lack of realism here, just as there is a lack of biblical faithfulness. The universalists' dream—fantasy, rather—is in truth a kite that will not fly. The questions for them: Why does God allow multitudes to go to hell before he calls them to faith? More searchingly, why do Jesus and the apostles give no hint that God intends to lead every member of this fallen human race to heaven? Why do they speak instead as if each person's decisions made here determine their state hereafter?

Is there not something heretical about the universalist account of God's love, which parts company with the Bible so radically?

## IN CONCLUSION

To critique a speculative hypothesis that, however well meant, seeks to be wiser than the Word of God gives no pleasure. We have, however, done it, and this is what we have found: Universalism does not stand up to biblical examination. Its sunny optimism may be reassuring and comfortable, but it wholly misses the tragic quality of human sin, human unbelief, and human death set forth in the Bible.

Furthermore, its inevitable weakening of the motive for evangelism is subversive of the church's mission, given to us by Jesus. Universalism reinvents, and thereby distorts, biblical teaching about God and salvation. It needs to be actively opposed so that the world may know the truth about the judgment, the love, and the salvation of our God.

# PREACHING HELL IN A TOLERANT AGE

## TIMOTHY KELLER

[Originally published in the Fall 1997 issue of *Leadership*; adapted and reprinted with permission.]

THE YOUNG MAN IN MY OFFICE was impeccably dressed and articulate. An Ivy League MBA, successful in the financial world, he had lived in three countries before age thirty. Raised in a family with only a loose connection to a mainline church, he had little understanding of Christianity.

I was therefore gratified to learn of his intense spiritual interest, recently piqued as he attended our church. He said he was ready to embrace the gospel. But there was a final obstacle.

"You've said that if we do not believe in Christ," he said, "we are lost and condemned. I'm sorry, I just cannot buy that. I work with some fine people who are Muslim, Jewish, or agnostic. I cannot believe they are going to hell just because they don't believe in Jesus. In fact, I cannot reconcile the very idea of hell with a loving God—even if he is holy."

This young man expressed what may be the most common objection contemporary people make to the Christian message. (A close second, in my experience, is the problem of suffering and evil.) Many today cannot accept the idea of final judgment and hell.

Thus, it's tempting to avoid such topics in our preaching. But neglecting unpleasant doctrines of the historic faith will often bring about counterintuitive consequences. There is an ecological balance to scriptural truth that we cannot risk disturbing.

If an area is cleared of its predatory or undesirable animals, the balance of that environment may be so upset that desirable plants and animals are also lost—through overbreeding with a limited food supply. The unwanted predator that was eliminated actually kept in balance the number of other animals and plants necessary to that particular ecosystem. In the same way, if we avoid difficult or "harsh" doctrines within the historic Christian faith, we may find, to our surprise, that we have gutted pleasant and cherished beliefs, too.

In the end, the loss of the doctrines of hell, judgment, and the holiness of God does irreparable damage to our deepest comforts—particularly our understanding of God's grace and love, and of human dignity and our value to him. To preach the good news, we must also preach the bad.

But in this age of tolerance, how?

## HOW TO PREACH HELL TO TRADITIONALISTS

Before preaching on the subject of hell, we must recognize that most congregations are made up of two groups. At the risk of oversimplifying, we'll call them traditionalists and secularists. These two groups hear the message of hell completely differently.

People with a traditional mind-set tend to have a belief in God, a strong sense of moral absolutes, and an understanding of the obligation to do good. These people are often older, from strong Catholic or religious Jewish backgrounds, from conservative evangelical/Pentecostal Protestant backgrounds, or first-generation immigrants from non-European countries.

The way to show traditionally minded persons their need for the gospel is by simply saying, "Your sin separates you from God! You can't be righteous enough for him." Imperfection is the duty-worshiper's horror. Traditionalists are motivated toward God in order to escape punishment in hell. They sense the seriousness of sin.

However, traditionalists may respond to the gospel only out of fear, unless we show them Jesus experienced not only pain on the cross but also hell itself. This must be held up so they are attracted to Christ for the beauty of the costly love of his sacrifice. To the traditionally minded person, hell must be presented as the surest proof of how much Christ loved you.

Here is one way I have preached this:

> Until we come to grips with this terrible doctrine, we will never begin to understand the depths of what Jesus did for us on the cross. His body was being destroyed in the worst possible way, but that was a fleabite compared to what was happening to his soul. When he cried out that his God had forsaken him, he was experiencing hell itself.
>
> If a mild acquaintance denounces you or rejects you, it hurts. If a good friend does the same, the hurt is far worse. However, if your spouse walks out on you, saying, "I never want to see you again," that is far more devastating still. The longer, deeper, and more intimate the relationship, the more torturous is any separation.
>
> The Son's relationship with the Father was without beginning and infinitely greater than the most intimate and passionate human relationship. When Jesus was cut off from God, he went into the deepest pit and the most powerful furnace of suffering, one beyond all imagining. And he did it voluntarily—he did it for us.

## HOW TO PREACH HELL TO SECULARISTS

In contrast to the traditionalist, the person with a secular mind-set is offended by the idea of hell. Such individuals tend to have (1) only a vague belief in the divine, if any; (2) suspicion of moral absolutes; and (3) a sense of obligation to be true to their dreams. They tend to be younger, from nominal Catholic or nonreligious Jewish backgrounds, from liberal Protestant backgrounds, residents of urban or educated areas, or immigrants from Western Europe or parts of Asia.

When preaching hell to people of this mind-set, I've found I must make four arguments.

## 1. Sin Is Slavery

I do not define sin as just breaking rules but also as "making something besides God our ultimate source of value and worth." These good things, which become idols, enslave us mentally and spiritually and drive us relentlessly, even to hell if we let them.

I say, "You are actually being religious, though you don't know it—you are seeking to find a kind of salvation through things that end up controlling you in a destructive way." Slavery is the choice-worshiper's horror.

C. S. Lewis's imagining of hell can be helpful for secularists. In *The Great Divorce*, Lewis describes a busload of people from hell who come to the outskirts of heaven. In the story, they are urged to leave behind the sins that have trapped them in hell. Lewis's descriptions of people in hell are striking because they mirror the denial and self-delusion of substance abusers. When addicted to alcohol or an idol like success or money, we are miserable, but we blame others and pity ourselves; we do not take responsibility for our behavior or see the roots of our problem. Lewis writes:

> Hell ... begins with a grumbling mood, and yourself still distinct from it: perhaps even criticizing it.... You can repent and come out of it again. But there may come a day when you can do that no longer. Then there will be no you left to criticize the mood or even enjoy it, but just the grumble itself going on forever like a machine.

Many people today struggle with the idea of God's punishing disobedient people. When sin is seen as slavery, and hell—in one sense—as the freely chosen eternal slum of the universe, hell becomes much more comprehensible.

Here is an example of how I try to explain this:

> First, sin separates us from the presence of God (Isa. 59:2), which is the source of all joy (Ps. 16:11), love, wisdom, or good thing of any sort (James 1:17).

Second, to understand hell we must understand sin as slavery. Romans 1:21–25 tells us that we were built to live for God supremely, but instead we live for love, work, achievement, or morality to give us meaning and worth. Thus every person, religious or not, is worshiping something—idols, pseudo-saviors—to get their worth. But these things enslave us with guilt (if we fail to attain them), or anger (if someone blocks them from us), or fear (if they are threatened), or drivenness (since we must have them). Guilt, anger, fear, and drivenness are like fire that destroys us. Sin is worshiping anything but Jesus—and the wages of sin is slavery.

Perhaps the greatest paradox of all is that the people on Lewis's bus from hell are enslaved because they freely choose to be. They would rather have their freedom (as they define it) than salvation. Their tragic delusion is that if they glorified God, they would lose their human greatness (Gen. 3:4–5), but in reality their choice has ruined their human greatness. Hell is, as Lewis says, "the greatest monument to human freedom."

## 2. Hell Is No More Exclusive Than Tolerance

Nothing is more characteristic of the contemporary mind-set than the statement: "I think Christ is fine, but I also believe a devout Muslim or Buddhist or even a good atheist will certainly find God." A slightly different version is: "I don't think God would send a person who lives a good life to hell just for holding the wrong belief." This view is generally seen as inclusive.

In preaching about hell, then, I seek to counter this mind-set in the following way:

> The universal religion of humankind is: We develop a good record and give it to God, and then he owes us. The gospel is: God develops a good record and gives it to us, and then we owe him (Rom. 1:17). In short, to say a good person can find God is to say good behavior is the way to God.
>
> In essence this view says, "Good people can find God, but bad people cannot." But what happens to us moral failures? We are

excluded. You see, you can believe that people are saved by goodness or you can believe that people are saved by God's grace, but you cannot believe both at once—and the approach that appears inclusive at first glance is really equally exclusive.

The gospel says, "People who know they aren't good can find God, and people who think they are good cannot." Those who believe their moral efforts can help them reach God are excluded.

So both gospel and the secularist's approach are exclusive, but the gospel's is the more inclusive exclusivity. It says joyfully, "It doesn't matter who you are or what you've done. It doesn't matter if you've been at the gates of hell. You can be welcomed and embraced fully and instantly through Christ."

## 3. Christianity's View of Hell Is More Personal Than the Alternative View

Fairly often I meet people who say, "I have a personal relationship with a loving God, yet I don't believe in Jesus Christ at all."

"Why not?" I ask.

They reply, "Because God is too loving to pour out infinite suffering on anyone for sin."

But their answer raises another set of questions, namely: "Did it cost God anything to love us and embrace us? Did he agonize or cry out for us? What else is lost if we lose Jesus' nails and thorns?"

Their answer usually is: "I don't think any of that was necessary."

How unsatisfying this is in the end. In an effort to make God more loving, we often make God less loving. His love, in this understanding, required no action. It was sentimentality, not love at all. The worship of a God like this will always end up being impersonal, cognitive, and ethical. There will be no joyful self-abandonment, no humble boldness, no constant sense of wonder. We would not sing to such a being, "Love so amazing, so divine, demands my soul, my life, my all."

This more "sensitive" approach to the subject of hell is actually impersonal. It says, "It doesn't matter if you believe in the person of Christ, as long as you follow his example."

But to say that is to say the essence of religion is intellectual and ethical, not personal. To say that any good person can find God is to create a religion without tears, without experience, without contact.

The gospel is not less than an understanding of biblical truths and principles, but it is infinitely more. The essence of salvation is knowing a Person (John 17:3). As with knowing any person, there is repenting and weeping and rejoicing and encountering. The gospel calls us to a wildly passionate, intimate love relationship with Jesus Christ, and it calls that "the core of true salvation."

## 4. There Is No Love without Wrath

What rankles many people today is the wrath of God: "I can't believe in a God who sends people to suffer eternally. What kind of a loving God is filled with wrath?"

So in preaching about hell, we must explain that a God without wrath is a God without love. Here's how I tried to do that in one sermon:

> People ask, "What kind of a loving God could be filled with wrath?" But any loving person is often filled with wrath. In *Hope Has Its Reasons*, Becky Pippert writes, "Think how we feel when we see someone we love ravaged by unwise actions or relationships. Do we respond with benign tolerance as we might toward strangers? Far from it.... Anger isn't the opposite of love. Hate is, and the final form of hate is indifference."
>
> Pippert then quotes E. H. Gifford, "Human love here offers a true analogy: the more a father loves his son, the more he hates in him the drunkard, the liar, the traitor."
>
> She concludes: "If I, a flawed, narcissistic, sinful woman, can feel this much pain and anger over someone's condition, how much more a morally perfect God who made them? God's wrath is not a cranky explosion, but his settled opposition to the cancer of sin which is eating out the insides of the human race he loves with his whole being."

This is why faithful and balanced preaching on this subject must depict hell as both the result of a human choice (as "the greatest monument to human freedom") *and* of divine judgment. God must, and does, actively judge and reject those who have rejected him.

## A GOD LIKE THIS

Once, following a sermon on the parable of Lazarus and the rich man, the post-service question-and-answer session focused on the subject of eternal judgment. My heart sank when a young college student said, "I've gone to church all my life, but I don't think I can believe in a God like this." Her tone was more sad than defiant, but her willingness to stay and talk showed that her mind was open.

Usually in these sessions, all the questions were pitched to me, and I would respond as best I could. But on this occasion people began answering one another.

An elderly businesswoman said, "Well, I'm not much of a church-goer, and I'm in some shock now. I always disliked the very idea of hell, but I never thought about it as a measure of what God was willing to endure in order to love me."

Then a mature Christian made a connection with a sermon a month before on Jesus at Lazarus's tomb in John 11. "The text tells us that Jesus wept," he said, "yet he was also extremely angry at evil. That's helped me. He is not just an angry God or a weeping, loving God — he's both. He doesn't only judge evil, but he also takes the hell and judgment himself for us on the cross."

The second woman nodded, "Yes. I always thought hell told me about how angry God was with us, but I didn't know it also told me about how much he was willing to suffer and weep for us. I never knew how much hell told me about Jesus' love. It's very moving."

Indeed, it is only because of the doctrine of judgment and hell that Jesus' proclamation of grace and love are so brilliant and astounding. May we never lose sight of either in our preaching.

# CONCLUSION

## CHRISTOPHER W. MORGAN
## AND ROBERT A. PETERSON

HELL IS BEING QUESTIONED TODAY, even by evangelicals. The idea that God would punish all people who do not trust in Christ is decidedly unpopular. It would be easier for all of us to downplay it. After all, hell repels moderns and postmoderns alike. It implies that Christians are narrow-minded and intolerant.

In a sense, hell stands for everything our contemporary culture rejects — that God's love is interconnected with his justice, that humans are sinful by nature and by choice, that Jesus is the only Savior, that faith in him is the only way to be right with God, and that all sin will ultimately be punished. To speak of hell in today's world truly is precarious.

However, what is the alternative? Not to speak of hell? As this book has shown, that is not an option for God's people because God's Word clearly teaches it. Every New Testament author speaks of the future punishment of the wicked. Jesus himself stands out as hell's chief defender — no medieval preacher ever spoke as fearsomely about the horrors of hell as Jesus did. Those of us who call Jesus our Lord do not have the privilege of rejecting a teaching he so emphatically repeated.

Christians also must embrace the doctrine of hell because of its prominent place in a biblical worldview. The doctrine of hell does not appear in isolation in the Bible; it is linked to the indispensible doctrines of God, sin, and the atonement.

Hell emerges from a biblical understanding of God. It reminds us that though God's love is central, it should not be viewed independently of his other attributes. His love is in unity with his justice and his holiness. God's love is not sentimental, but a holy love and a just love. Therefore, God's love should not be viewed as an obstacle to his willingness to see justice executed.

Hell is also connected to a biblical understanding of humanity and sin. Hell reminds us that being human comes with awesome privileges and awesome responsibilities. To choose sin rather than God is a high crime. The words of medieval theologian Anselm to his student Boso are worth remembering: "You have not yet considered the gravity of your sin." Fundamentally, hell can only be understood as God's just punishment on sin.

Yet hell is also a tragedy. It is tragic that sin entered the world through Adam, that humans continue to rebel against God, and that sinners reject the Savior. In this sense, the horror of hell *should* offend our moral sensibilities. Even more so, the suffering of those in hell should break our hearts—not only because of the dreadfulness of the punishment but also because of the awfulness of sin, the crime that demands such a penalty. The problem is not hell, nor is it God. Sin is the problem, and it is what should repulse us.

The biblical doctrine of hell is also linked to Jesus' death. Fully God and fully human, Jesus died on the cross as the only substitute for our sin. He bore the penalty of sin for every believer. But those who fail to come to Christ in faith and repentance will have to pay that penalty themselves. In other words, just as there are only two options available for sinners (to receive forgiveness from Christ or to be punished eternally), there are only two ways to gauge the horror of sin—by reflecting on the cross and by considering hell.

Furthermore, the doctrines of God, sin, and the atonement are themselves interwoven and can only be understood fully in light of hell. Let us explain. First, only when we recognize God's holiness will we be able to fully understand the horror of sin. Second, only when we become aware of the awfulness of our sin will we sense the dreadfulness of hell and the price of Christ's death. Third, only when we grapple with the punishment of hell and the extent of Christ's atoning death can we begin to grasp God's amazing grace. Clearly, hell is an integral part of Christian theology.

As such, it must be on the lips of those who want to be faithful to Jesus and his Word. To speak of hell is precarious. But not to speak of hell is more precarious. God our Judge requires us to proclaim the whole truth about him, and we owe it to fellow sinners to tell them the unabridged story of his love and forgiveness. That way they too can better understand their desperate need for forgiveness and experience the joy found only in knowing Christ.

Our prayer is that you will join us and countless Christians throughout history and around the world in sharing the whole counsel of God—including hell—with Christians and non-Christians alike. May we do it with a passionate love for the Lord Jesus, abiding conviction in the truthfulness of God's Word, and heartfelt compassion for the lost.

# FURTHER READING

Blanchard, John. *Whatever Happened to Hell?* Durham, England: Evangelical Press, 1993.

Davies, Eryl. *An Angry God? What the Bible Says about Wrath, Final Judgment, and Hell.* Bridgend, Wales: Evangelical Press of Wales, 1991.

Dixon, Larry. *The Other Side of the Good News: Confronting the Contemporary Challenges to Jesus' Teaching on Hell.* Great Britain: Christian Focus, 2003.

Fernando, Ajith. *Crucial Questions about Hell.* Wheaton, IL: Crossway, 1994.

Fudge, Edward William, and Robert A. Peterson. *Two Views of Hell: A Biblical and Theological Dialogue.* Downers Grove, IL: InterVarsity Press, 2000.

Kistler, Don, ed. *The Wrath of Almighty God: Jonathan Edwards on God's Judgment against Sinners.* Morgan, PA: Soli Deo Gloria, 1996.

Milne, Bruce. *The Message of Heaven and Hell: Grace and Destiny.* The Bible Speaks Today. Downers Grove, IL: InterVarsity Press, 2002.

Morgan, Christopher W. *Jonathan Edwards and Hell.* Great Britain: Christian Focus, 2004.

———, and Robert A. Peterson, eds. *Faith Comes by Hearing: A Response to Inclusivism.* Downers Grove, IL: InterVarsity Press, 2008.

———, and Robert A. Peterson, eds. *Hell under Fire: Modern Scholarship Reinvents Eternal Punishment.* Grand Rapids: Zondervan, 2004.

———, and Robert A. Peterson. *What Is Hell?* Basics of the Faith. Phillipsburg, NJ: P&R Publishing, 2010.

Packer, James I. "The Problem of Eternal Punishment." *Evangel: The British Evangelical Review* 10 (Summer 1992): 13–19. Orig. published in *Crux* 26 (Summer 1990): 18–25.

Peterson, Robert A. *Hell on Trial: The Case for Eternal Punishment.* Phillipsburg, NJ: P&R Publishing, 1995.

Shedd, William G. T. *The Doctrine of Endless Punishment.* New York: Charles Scribner's Sons, 1886; reprint, Minneapolis: Klock & Klock, 1980.

Strachan, Owen, and Doug Sweeney. *Jonathan Edwards on Heaven and Hell.* Chicago: Moody Press, 2010.

# NOTES

1. *Time* magazine (April 25, 2011).
2. David Lodge, *Souls and Bodies* (London: Penguin, 1980), 113.
3. Quoted in Richard Marius, *Martin Luther: The Christian between God and Death* (Cambridge, MA: Harvard Univ. Press, 1999), 60.
4. Jonathan Edwards, "The Torments of Hell Are Exceedingly Great," in *Sermons and Discourses, 1723–1729*, ed. Kenneth P. Minkema (The Works of Jonathan Edwards, vol. 14; New Haven, CT: Yale Univ. Press, 1997), 326.
5. D. P. Walker, *The Decline of Hell: Seventeenth-Century Discussions of Eternal Torment* (London: Routledge & Kegan Paul, 1964), 77.
6. Cited by Jaroslav Pelikan, "Christian Doctrine and Modern Culture (Since 1700)," in *The Christian Tradition: A History of the Development of Doctrine* (Chicago: Univ. of Chicago Press, 1989), 5:177.
7. Ibid., 5:178.
8. Cited in Geoffrey Rowell, *Hell and the Victorians: A Study of the Nineteenth-Century Theological Controversies Concerning Eternal Punishment and the Future Life* (Oxford: Clarendon, 1974), 212.
9. As cited by A. N. Wilson, *God's Funeral: A Biography of Faith and Doubt in Western Civilization* (New York: Random House, 1999), 9.
10. Lewis Carroll, "Eternal Punishment," in *The Lewis Carroll Picture Book*, ed. Stuart Dodgson Collingwood (London: T. Fisher Unwon, 1899), 345–55.
11. Frederic W. Farrar, *Eternal Hope: Five Sermons* (London: Macmillan, 1904), 68–69.
12. Rowell, *Hell and the Victorians*, vii.
13. Rudolf Bultmann, *Jesus Christ and Mythology* (New York: Charles Scribner's Sons, 1958), 36.
14. Jürgen Moltmann, *Experiences in Theology: Ways and Forms of Christian Theology* (Minneapolis: Fortress, 2000), 241–42.
15. Charles H. Spurgeon, "Paul's First Prayer," a sermon preached March 25, 1855, at Exeter Hall in London, *The New Park Street Pulpit* (London: Passmore and Alabaster, 1856), 124.
16. Charles H. Spurgeon, "The Resurrection of the Dead," a sermon preached February 17, 1856, at New Park Street Chapel, Southwark (London: Passmore and Alabaster, 1857), 104.

17. John Wenham, *The Goodness of God* (Downers Grove, IL: InterVarsity Press, 1974), 27.

18. Ibid., 37–38.

19. John Wenham, *Facing Hell: An Autobiography* (London: Paternoster, 1998), 230. The 1991 date refers to a paper Wenham presented to an audience at Rutherford House, Edinburgh, in that year.

20. David L. Edwards and John R. W. Stott, *Evangelical Essentials: A Liberal-Evangelical Dialogue* (Downers Grove, IL: InterVarsity Press, 1988), 318.

21. Os Guinness, *The Gravedigger File* (Downers Grove, IL: InterVarsity Press, 1983), 92.

22. C. S. Lewis, "The Humanitarian Theory of Punishment," in *God in the Dock: Essays on Theology and Ethics*, ed. Walter Hooper (Grand Rapids: Eerdmans, 1970), 288.

23. Kimon Howland Sargeant, *Seeker Churches: Promoting Traditional Religion in a Nontraditional Way* (New Brunswick, NJ: Rutgers Univ. Press, 2000), 198.

24. Scot McKnight, *A New Vision for Israel* (Grand Rapids: Eerdmans, 1999), 139.

25. Moses Stuart, *Exegetical Essays on Several Words Relating to Future Punishment* (Philadelphia: Presbyterian Publication Committee, 1867 [reprint of 1830 edition]), 62; Stuart's emphasis throughout.

26. McKnight, *A New Vision for Israel*, 38.

27. Edward W. Fudge and Robert A. Peterson, *Two Views of Hell* (Downers Grove, IL: InterVarsity Press, 2000), 20; see also 82.

28. Ibid., 43–44.

29. Peter Head, "Duration of Divine Judgment," in *Eschatology in Bible and Theology: Evangelical Essays at the Dawn of a New Millennium* (ed. Kent E. Brower and Mark W. Elliott; Downers Grove, IL: InterVarsity Press, 1997), 223–34.

30. J. N. D. Kelly, *Early Christian Doctrines* (rev. ed.; New York: Harper & Row, 1978), 466.

31. Cited in Tony Gray, "The Nature of Hell," *Eschatology in Bible and Theology*, ed. Brower and Elliot, 233–34; see also Edwards and Stott, *Evangelical Essentials*, 314.

32. See sec. 1 of the December 2, 2001, *Chicago Tribune*.

33. Paul Watson, "Taliban Justice: Public Executions and Amputations," in ibid., 9. Other portions of Watson's report are even more harrowing.

34. For an insightful evaluation of Paul's teaching on hell, including an even-handed treatment of Pauline passages often cited in defense of universalism, see Douglas J. Moo, "Paul on Hell," *Hell under Fire: Modern Scholarship Reinvents Eternal Punishment* (ed. Christopher W. Morgan and Robert A. Peterson; Grand Rapids: Zondervan, 2004), 91–109.

35. See Christopher W. Morgan, *A Theology of James: Wisdom for God's People*, (Explorations in Biblical Theology; Phillipsburg, NJ: P&R Publishing, 2010), 164–68.

# NOTES

36. See also Gregory K. Beale, in "The Revelation on Hell," in *Hell under Fire*, 111–34.

37. See Moo, "Paul on Hell," 105.

38. Ibid.

39. See Kendall S. Harmon, "The Case against Conditionalism: A Response to Edward William Fudge," in *Universalism and the Doctrine of Hell: Papers Presented at the Fourth Edinburgh Conference on Christian Dogmatics, 1991* (ed. Nigel M. de S. Cameron; Grand Rapids: Baker, 1992), 220–24.

40. Augustine, *Enchiridion* 112, in *The Works of Aurelius Augustine* (Edinburgh: T&T Clark, 1873), 9:254. Quoted in Harmon, "The Case against Conditionalism," 220.

41. Harmon, "The Case against Conditionalism," 213.

42. John H. Gerstner, *Repent or Perish: With a Special Reference to the Conservative Attack on Hell* (Ligonier, PA: Soli Deo Gloria, 1990), 189–90.

43. Madeleine L'Engle, *The Irrational Season* (New York: Seabury, 1977), 97.

44. Barth holds that through and in Jesus Christ all humankind has been and now actually is redeemed, and faith is simply believing this to be the truth about oneself. But, fearing it would infringe upon God's freedom should he speak of the destiny of unbelievers, Barth takes "no position for or against" universalism—no dogmatic position, that is (*The Humanity of God* [Richmond, VA: John Knox, 1960], 61). Wishfully, however, he says: "Universal salvation remains an open possibility for which we may hope" (*Church Dogmatics* IV.3 [Edinburgh: T&T Clark, 1961], 478). His unwillingness to embrace dogmatic universalism is deeply problematical, for his insistence on the factuality of every person's actual redemption makes it seem as if the divine freedom he wants to safeguard is simply God's freedom to not take his own achievement in Christ seriously—which is, of course, unthinkable.

45. Basil Mitchell, *The Justification of Religious Belief* (London: Macmillan, 1973), 19.

46. Exponents of "open theism" lay great weight on this inference; it is the point on which the entire pyramid of their thought seems to be balanced. It is remarkable how little awareness they show of the analogical nature of biblical language.

47. See Harold A. Netland, *Dissonant Voices: Religious Pluralism and the Question of Truth* (Grand Rapids: Eerdmans, 1991), 10. Netland refers to John Hick's *Myth of God Incarnate* (Maryknoll, NY: Orbis, 1987).

48. John Hick, *An Interpretation of Religion* (New Haven, CT: Yale Univ. Press, 1989), 240.

49. O. C. Quick, *The Gospel of the New World* (London: Nisbet, 1944), 116.

50. W. G. T. Shedd, *Dogmatic Theology* (Edinburgh: T&T Clark, 1889), 2:680.

51. Emil Brunner, *Eternal Hope* (London: Lutterworth, 1954), 183.

52. Nels Ferré, *The Christian Understanding of God* (London: SCM, 1951), 230.

# NOTES

53. Ibid.
54. See J. Hastings, ed., *Dictionary of Christ and the Gospels* (Edinburgh: T&T Clark, 1908), 2:785.
55. John Sanders, *No Other Name* (Grand Rapids: Eerdmans, 1992), 97, with reference to Friedrich Schleiermacher, *The Christian Faith* (ed. and trans. H. R. Mackintosh and J. S. Stewart; Edinburgh: T&T Clark, 1928), 721.

# CONTRIBUTORS

**Timothy Keller** is senior pastor at Redeemer Presbyterian Church, Manhattan: and *New York Times* bestselling author of *The Reason for God*. He is also author of *Counterfeit Gods* and *The Prodigal God* book, film, and discussion guide.

**R. Albert Mohler, Jr.** (PhD, Southern Baptist Theological Seminary), is president and professor of Christian theology at Southern Baptist Theological Seminary in Louisville, Kentucky.

**J. I. Packer** (DPhil, Oxford University) is a member of the board of governors and professor of theology at Regent College, Vancouver, British Columbia.

**Robert W. Yarbrough** (PhD, University of Aberdeen) is chair and professor of New Testament at Trinity Evangelical Divinity School in Deerfield, Illinois.

# Counterpoints: Bible and Theology Three Views on the Rapture

Pretribulation, Prewrath, or Posttribulation

*Craig Blaising, Alan Hultberg, and Douglas J. Moo; Alan Hultberg, General Editor; Stanley N. Gundry, Series Editor*

The rapture, or the belief that, at some point, Jesus' living followers will join him forever while others do not, is an important but contested doctrine among evangelicals. Scholars generally hold one of three perspectives on the timing of and circumstances surrounding the rapture, all of which are presented in *Three Views on the Rapture*. The recent prominence of a Pre-Wrath understanding of the rapture calls for a fresh examination of this important but contested Christian belief.

Alan D. Hultberg (PhD, Trinity International University and professor of New Testament at Talbot School of Theology) explains the Pre-Wrath view; Craig Blaising (PhD, Dallas Theological Seminary and president of Southwestern Baptist Theological Seminary) defends the Pre-Tribulation view; and Douglas Moo (PhD, University of St. Andrews and professor of New Testament at Wheaton College) sets forth the Post-Tribulation view. Each author provides a substantive explanation of his position, which is critiqued by the other two authors. A thorough introduction gives a historical overview of the doctrine of the rapture and its effects on the church.

The interactive and fair-minded format of the Counterpoints series allows readers to consider the strengths and weaknesses of each view and draw informed, personal conclusions.

*Available in stores and online!*

# Gospel in Life Discussion Guide with DVD

## Grace Changes Everything

*Timothy Keller*

Pack containing one softcover guide and one DVD. Join author and pastor Tim Keller in an eight-week, video-based study of the gospel and how to live it out in everyday life. In Week One you and your group will study the city, our home now—the world, that is. Week Eight closes with the theme of the eternal city, our heavenly home—the world that is to come. In between, you'll learn how the gospel changes our hearts, our community, and how we live in this world. *Gospel in Life* is an invitation to all who seek to live the message of Jesus right here and right now ... in our hearts, in our homes, and in the community around us.

Session titles include:

Session 1, The City—The World That Is
Session 2, Heart—Three Ways to Live
Session 3, Idolatry—The Sin beneath the Sin
Session 4, Community
Session 5, Witness—An Alternate City
Session 6, Work—-Cultivating the Garden
Session 7-Justice—A People for Others
Session 8, Eternity—The World That Is to Come

*Available in stores and online!*

**ZONDERVAN®**
.com

# The Reason for God Discussion Guide with DVD

## Conversations on Faith and Life

*Timothy Keller*

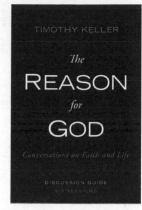

Pastor and author Timothy Keller meets with a group of skeptics over six sessions to debate their doubts and questions about Christianity. Using literature, philosophy, real-life experiences and constant reference to the Bible, Keller explains how the belief in a Christian God is a sound and rational one. Filmed live and unscripted as Keller interacts with the group, this curriculum models the way in which Christians can address the six most common questions from skeptics. It also provides the resources for Christians to meet with their own group.

Session Titles and Descriptions

1. How can there be only one true religion?
2. Why does God allow suffering?
3. How could a loving God sent people to Hell?
4. Hasn't science disproved Christianity?
5. How can you take the Bible literally?
6. What is Christianity all about?

*Available in stores and online!*

# Surprised by Hope
# Participant's Guide
# with DVD

## Rethinking Heaven, the Resurrection, and the Mission of the Church

*N.T. Wright*

Gain an exciting new vision for your life on earth in light of your future in heaven.

Wonderful as is the promise of heaven, a glorious hereafter is just part of what salvation is about. What about today? Jesus called his followers the salt of the earth and the light of the world. Your life here and now is of tremendous consequence, and what you believe about the future has a direct impact on how you live in the present.

In six transforming, faith-inspiring sessions, premier biblical scholar N. T. Wright opens your eyes to the amazing full scope of what God's Word has to say about the world to come and the world that is.

Filled with discussion questions, thoughts for reflection, and ideas for personal application, this study guide will help you get the most out of each session as you explore such questions as

- What is heaven really like?
- Is our main duty as Christians simply to help non-Christians get there?
- What hope does the gospel hold for this present life?
- In what ways does God intend for us to experience that hope personally and spread its healing power to the world around us?

*Surprised by Hope* will give you a clearer vision both of the future and of God's kingdom at hand today.

*Available in stores and online!*

# Hell Under Fire

## Modern Scholarship Reinvents Eternal Punishment

*Christopher W. Morgan
and Robert A. Peterson,
General Editors*

Of all the teachings of Christianity, the doctrine of hell is easily the most troubling, so much so that in recent years the church has been quietly tucking it away. Rarely mentioned anymore in the pulpit, it has faded through disuse among evangelicals and been attacked by liberal theologians. Hell is no longer only the target of those outside the church. Today, a disturbing number of professing Christians question it as well. Perhaps more than at any other time in history, hell is under fire.

The implications of the historic view of hell make the popular alternatives, annihilationism and universalism, seem extremely appealing. But the bottom line is still God's Word. What does the Old Testament reveal about hell? What does Paul the apostle have to say, or the book of Revelation? Most important, what does Jesus, the ultimate expression of God's love, teach us about God's wrath?

Hell may be under fire, but its own flames cannot be quenched by popular opinion. This book helps us gain a biblical perspective on what hell is and why we cannot afford to ignore it. And it offers us a better understanding of the One who longs for all people to escape judgment and obtain eternal life through Jesus Christ.

## Share Your Thoughts

**With the Author:** Your comments will be forwarded to the author when you send them to *zauthor@zondervan.com*.

**With Zondervan:** Submit your review of this book by writing to *zreview@zondervan.com*.

## Free Online Resources at
## www.zondervan.com

**Zondervan AuthorTracker:** Be notified whenever your favorite authors publish new books, go on tour, or post an update about what's happening in their lives at www.zondervan.com/authortracker.

**Daily Bible Verses and Devotions:** Enrich your life with daily Bible verses or devotions that help you start every morning focused on God. Visit www.zondervan.com/newsletters.

**Free Email Publications:** Sign up for newsletters on Christian living, academic resources, church ministry, fiction, children's resources, and more. Visit www.zondervan.com/newsletters.

**Zondervan Bible Search:** Find and compare Bible passages in a variety of translations at www.zondervanbiblesearch.com.

**Other Benefits:** Register to receive online benefits like coupons and special offers, or to participate in research.

**ZONDERVAN**.com/
**AUTHORTRACKER**
*follow your favorite authors*